Building A Strong Marriage & Family

With Style and Integrity

by
W. Blair Slaughter, Jr.

MARRIAGE MINISTRIES
Cornerstone

BUILDING A STRONG MARRIAGE AND FAMILY

© 2002 W. Blair Slaughter, Jr.

International Standard Book Number 0-9715355-0-7

ALL RIGHTS RESERVED
No part of this book may be reproduced or transmitted in any form or by any means, electronic or mechanical, including photocopying, recording or by any information storage or retrieval system, without permission in writing from the publisher. Permission to quote brief excerpts for review purposes is granted without further permission when accompanied by publication data.

Cover Photo by Anne Grant Photography

Printed in thee United States of America

Scripture taken from the New American Standard Bible ©, Copyright © 1960, 1962, 1963, 1968, 1971, 1972, 1973, 1975,1977, 1995 by the Lockman Foundation. Used by permission.

Also quoted The Amplified New Testament (AMP) copyright © 1958, 1987 by The Lockman Foundation and The New International Version (NIV) © 1978 by the New York International Bible Society. Used by permission.

DISCLAIMER: The purpose of this book is to provide insights regarding Scriptural truths for application in the reader's marriage and family relationship. It is not meant to replace professional counseling for emotional or psychological disturbances. Referral to a qualified counselor or therapist is recommended for issues outside the scope of this publication, which is intended only for general use, and not as a specific course of treatment.

Published by Cornerstone Marriage Ministries, Inc.
Post Office Box 5721
High Point, NC 27262-5721
336-887-2664
http://www.cornerstonemm.com

First Printing: July, 2002

Dedication

To Dr. Floyd McCallum, whose wise and Godly counsel not only gave my wife, Glenda, the courage to stand for the healing of our marriage but who was also used by God as an instrument to bring spiritual and emotional healing to my life and marriage.

To my wife Glenda, who with God's help displayed the following characteristics that enabled her to not give up on our marriage or me even though I walked out on her twice:

- Courage. When others tried to encourage her to date and forget about me, she refused. She was convinced our marriage was God's will and she courageously stood for that conviction in spite of what others said.

- Persistence. Glenda never gave up on me. She was convinced that God would lead me back home and that He still had a ministry for our lives. She constantly reminded me of this and persisted in her faith in God and in me. Once, during the separation, I asked her, "When will you accept the fact that this marriage is over?" She replied, "When God tells me it's over!"

- Gentleness. I was amazed how she could be so calm and peaceful when I saw her. During the entire ordeal, she displayed a gentleness that was not humanly possible.

- Genuine Love. For the first time in many years, I saw a love in her for me that I could not resist. How could she love and value me when I was treating her the way I was? It did not seem possible! I am fortunate to have a wife who was willing to lovingly stand by me until our marriage was back on solid ground.

To my oldest daughter, Shannon, who not only forgave me, but also allowed me the opportunity to earn her love and respect as her dad.

In loving memory of my youngest daughter, Amy, who not only forgave me and allowed me to earn her love and respect, but lived life in such a manner that she not only touched everyone she came in contact with, but left a lasting impression of her faith in God.

CONTENTS

PREFACE		9
FOREWORD		11
INTRODUCTION		13
PART ONE:	PRINCIPLES OF MARRIAGE	
Chapter 1	*Establishing Common Ground*	21
Chapter 2	*Defining Marriage*	25
PART TWO:	STRUCTURE OF MARRIAGE	
Chapter 3	*Leadership in Marriage*	29
Chapter 4	*Husbands, Love Your Wife As…*	41
Chapter 5	*Principles of Submission and Respect*	45
Chapter 6	*Biblical Priorities in Marriage*	49
PART THREE:	BONDING OF MARRIAGE	
Chapter 7	*Characteristics of Bonding*	65
Chapter 8	*Unresolved Issues with Parents*	73
Chapter 9	*Previous Relationships*	83
Chapter 10	*Premarital Sex*	87
Chapter 11	*Sexual Abuse*	99
Chapter 12	*Reasons for Marrying*	103
Chapter 13	*Abortion*	107
PART FOUR:	SPIRITUAL AND EMOTIONAL HEALING	
Chapter 14	*Restoring One's Value*	113

CONTENTS

Chapter 15 *Forgiveness: The Key to a Fulfilling Relationship* 121

PART FIVE: BUILDING A FAMILY TEAM

Chapter 16 *Recognize, Understand and Value Each Family Member* 137

Chapter 17 *Creating a Vision* 151

Chapter 18 *Develop a Mission Statement* 153

Chapter 19 *Establish Healthy Communication* 157

PART SIX: PARENTING

Chapter 20 *Christian Parents - Rebellious Children* 165

Chapter 21 *Guarding Your Children From Moral Impurity* ... 173

About W. Blair Slaughter, Jr. 179

Resources 181

Preface

I have by no means arrived to perfection. My journey has been one of tears, pain and disappointment. But, praise God, I have been delivered. This book is the story of my life. It is the story of God's Amazing Grace.

This book would never been written without the encouragement of faithful friends and family.

Thank you, David Emery, for being a faithful friend throughout the years. You planted the seed for this book several years ago by encouraging me to sit down and write my story.

Thank you, Dr. Tom Futrell, Richard Hardee, Jerry Pool, Lee Wolfe, Michael Gay, Robert Grills, Charles Reynolds, Rev. Alan Cox, and Frank Hensley for your serving as my board of directors and providing consistent encouragement.

Throughout my ministry, I felt there was a missing link. I finally discovered that link in understanding personality style blends and combinations. The training I have received under Dr. Robert Rohm, President of Personality Insights, is some of the greatest information I possess. Not only have you been an effective teacher and coach to me, but your input into Building a Family Team is invaluable. Thank you for being an inspiring motivator in my ministry.

Thank you, Anita Grills, for proof reading the original manuscript and offering your encouragement.

Thank you, Tracy Russo, for the time you spent pulling the sections together and editing the original manuscript.

Thank you, O'Nealya Gronstal, for your editing skills needed to bring this book to finality. For the countless hours you spent making this book readable and for opening your home up for me to stay and work, thank you.

I owe a debt of gratitude to many people, all of whom I cannot remember, who have had an impact on my life and ministry. Only God knows when and where certain seeds were planted in my mind and therefore, I ask Him to bless all those who have influenced me on my journey.

Last, but not least, to all the couples I have worked with; I thank God because He has used each of you to teach me the valuable lessons that have, in turn, benefited the lives of many.

Foreword

I first met Blair Slaughter several years ago at a Personality Insights training seminar I conducted in Atlanta, GA. He seemed to be a friendly guy with a little "twinkle" in his eyes. (You know the look – like someone who knew the secret before everyone else had heard the news!) I liked Blair's positive attitude and happy spirit immediately.

Over the next few days, we had lunch and talked about issues relating to marriage, rearing children and the family in general. Blair had wisdom and insight way beyond his years. Since one of my passions is wisdom, I asked him where he learned all this information he was sharing with me. He told me he had not read it in a book. He had learned it through experience (the school I consider to be the best teacher, as well as the most real). He told me of the journey he had walked over the past few years. It was not a very pretty picture. Actually, it was ugly, hard and even cruel at times. As he shared his story, I was reminded of the story of the prodigal son. He ran from God, but God did not run from him.

Blair's story was strikingly real and honest, not like others I often heard that carefully omitted the painful details of a person's own rebellion and stupidity. He told me what he had put his wife, Glenda, through many times, as well as his two daughters. Anybody can make a mistake, but it takes a real man to admit those mistakes and then wake up and walk in a new direction.

I told Blair he needed to tell his story and share his wisdom in writing. The little "twinkle" in his eyes went away. He did not know how to do that. But, again, the mark of a real man is to walk in a new direction. So, he accepted the challenge and began the task. The book that you now hold in your hands is the result of his new walk. Blair has spent long hours working on this project so you will not have to go through everything he did. Part of wisdom is learning from the mistakes of others! As Blair completed this project I saw the "twinkle" return to his eyes. It should. This book will bring a "twinkle" to your eyes as well!

Again, what you are about to read is real and powerful. It will change your view of the way you view your marriage and family... for the better. I highly recommend this book. I trust it will have a wide audience. It is real. It is powerful. It is true.

God bless you,

Robert A. Rohm, President
Personality Insights, Inc.
Atlanta, GA

INTRODUCTION

While browsing through a Christian bookstore one day, I counted over 40 books pertaining to marriage, family and parenting. Two questions came to my mind. One, why are so many books written about these subjects? And two, what qualifies the authors to write these books, and what are their credentials?

Marriage and family is one of the most, if not the most, complex of all institutions in our society. No one book can address all the issues that one faces in the family unit. New books are published as a result of new research and the need to find more effective solutions to the problems that cause the destruction of the family unit.

Over the past nine years, I have read many books on the subject of marriage. I have found many of these books deal with what I call the "skills" of marriage. God taught me many principles that brought healing to my life and marriage through these books.

You may be asking yourself the same questions about me that I asked about other authors. Those are fair questions. In order to answer your questions, let me share my story with you.

I have been married to my wife for over 33 years and was a Senior Pastor for over 17 years. I earned a Master's Degree in Counseling and I have counseled literally hundreds of couples in the areas of marriage and family.. In addition to my credentials, you will read throughout the pages of this book my testimony of walking out on my wife and two daughters twice.

The principles I share in this book are the same ones that empowered me to heal my own marriage and family.

How It All Started

On Sunday, March 11, 1984, I stood behind the pulpit in the church I was pastoring, opened my Bible and read James 4:17 "Therefore, to one who knows the right things to do and does not do it, to him it is a sin." I closed my Bible and said to the congregation "The right thing for me to do is resign as your pastor, which I am now doing."

I walked off the platform and out the side door of the church. That was the beginning of four tumultuous years and some of the most trying experiences for my family and me.

These problems began very early in our marriage. However, being in the ministry, we felt we should not have problems, so we hid them in a closet. Soon there was not enough room in the closet to hide them all. By 1982,

I was so overwhelmed by these hidden problems; I was ready to walk away from the ministry and my marriage. However, that is when the first disaster struck. Our youngest daughter Amy, who was nine at the time, was diagnosed with Ewing's sarcoma, a bone cancer. The doctors gave only a 20 - 40 percent chance of recovery. Even though I was ready to walk out, I could not leave under those circumstances. I promised God, "If you get me through Amy's cancer, whether she lives or dies, I will then deal with my problems." God honored that prayer. In January 1984, when Amy finished her treatments and was cancer free, God reminded me of my promise but I (broke my promise and) decided to go my own way, taking matters into my own hands. At that point, I told my wife, Glenda, I was leaving the ministry. She soon began noticing a change in me, and one day she asked, "You don't love me anymore, do you?" I replied "No." The only way I knew to deal with my problems was to leave the ministry and my family, which I did on March 11, 1984The separation from my wife lasted three months. After a brief separation, we got back together for financially reasons. Believing that deep personal problems are due to spiritual problems, I made a new commitment to God during the last service of our district camp meeting on July 11, 198. I did not do anything else, however, to actively solve my problems at that time.

The next year went fairly well, but soon some of the same problems began to resurface. I struggled with issues, but could find no answers. I started going downhill both spiritually and emotionally. Lacking knowledge to deal with these vexing issues, my self-worth and value spiraled downward. As a result, I felt the marriage was over. The latter part of September 1986, I walked out on my wife and daughters for the second time, convinced the marriage was over for the last time. I will never forget the look on my daughters' faces when I told them I was leaving, again.

Glenda's story

When Blair left the first time, I was devastated. What was I going to do? I was dependent upon him. I did not have a job. The church was going to allow the girls and I to live in the parsonage until June. I had no idea were we would go after June. I pleaded with Blair to come back home, but he ignored my pleas. Upon the advice of a friend, I went to see a godly counselor. He was such an encouragement and was able to find the girls and myself a house to rent. When June arrived, Blair realized he could not support two households, so he came back home. Blair rededicated his life to the Lord and I thought everything was going to be back to normal. The next year was good for us as a couple and as a family. Then I noticed that Blair was not himself and realized he was in a personal struggle. As time went by, the changes were more noticeable. I had no idea of the severity of his inner battle. Now I can see that we made a tragic mistake believing our previous problems were spiritual. Due to this false belief, we did not seek counseling. Then came the terrible news a second time. He told me, "I'm leaving and this time it's for good." After Blair left the second time, I had mixed emotions. I felt rejection, hurt, anger, bitterness and guilt. I felt that God had deserted me. I wanted to give up- and who could blame me? Instead, God led me to Galatians 6:9, "And let us not lose heart in doing good, for in due time we shall reap if we do not grow weary (if we do not give up)."

Immediately, I went back to see the counselor I had previously seen. He told me that I could stand for the healing of my marriage even though Blair said it was over. It was my decision to make, and I decided in October to take a stand for our marriage. I knew it was God's will for our marriage to be healed because He said in His Word, "What therefore God has joined together, let no man separate" (Matthew 19:6b).

As I took a stand for our marriage, the Holy Spirit began to work on me through my counselor. As I examined my own heart, I admitted that I had contributed to our marital woes. As I dealt with these issues in my own life; I gained spiritual, physical, and emotional strength. I joined a support group at the counseling center where we fasted one day a week, praying for our personal needs, and the needs of each other's families.

Whenever I had contact with Blair, he would say, "You need to find yourself a good man, this marriage is over!" He seemed very cold and his heart was very hard. I would tell him I had a good man, he just did not know it, and God had a ministry for us. He just laughed at me.

God kept directing me to His Word. I would often wake up at night and pray, "Thank you Lord that you are creating within Blair a clean heart and renewing within him a right spirit." I found strength in prayer and God's Word.

It took several months for me to have a "resting faith" in God. I don't know how to explain it, except to say that when I totally committed my all to God, by telling Him that whatever He intended for my life I was willing to accept, I was then able to rest in Him and trust in His providence. I still had days when I felt rejected and lonely, but I had a divine peace in my heart.

It was not long after I had left my family the second time; I began to see a remarkable change in Glenda. I saw a side of her that I had never seen before. I liked the change but it made me angry. Why wasn't she like that before I left? She told me she was standing for our marriage. I ridiculed her and insisted that the marriage was over. Her reply to me was, "With me, the marriage isn't over until God tells me it's over." What really puzzled me was, how could she have this attitude when she knew I did not want the marriage?

When Glenda came to that "resting faith," the woman I was currently seeing dropped me like a hot potato. I was also fired from a very successful job. Deep down I knew God was working, but I continued to rebel. I was not going back into that marriage! I worked various jobs, and tried to get into other relationships with women, but with no success. I finally began to see God was working!

During this time, I went to church and still believed in God, but thought that He did not believe in me. I was convinced that He could help other people, but could not help me. Because I placed no value in myself, I did not believe God could value me either.

In September 1987, I found myself wanting my family back, but not the marriage. I knew I did not feel the love for Glenda that a husband should have for his wife and I felt unworthy of her love. There were nights I cried myself to sleep because I felt no one really cared about me. Of course, I know now that I was wrong.

In November, I decided to move out of an affordable apartment, and into a more expensive one with a co-worker whom I suspected was going to be fired from his job. I also knew that when he was fired, I could not afford the rent by myself. The week of Thanksgiving he was fired, so he moved backed to his hometown, leaving me with a lease I could not afford. Then God worked it out so I could get out of the lease. Because there was not an apartment available I could afford, I knew I needed to go back home. The question was, would Glenda take me back.

When I was visiting my daughters a couple weeks before Christmas, I asked Glenda what it would take to convince her the marriage was over. She replied, "When God tells me." That gave me the hope she would allow me to return. A few days later, I got up the nerve to tell her I needed to move back home until I got back on my feet. She cautiously sought the advice of her counselor before giving me an answer. He told her to let me move back home, trusting God to work on me in the process.

On January 1, 1988, I moved back home. Every weekend for the next two months, I went back to the city where I had previously lived for fifteen months. There I worked a weekend job and continued my rebellious lifestyle. Glenda did not say anything but her eyes and body language revealed hurt and pain each time I left.

During those two months, God used my past to show me what I was and used Glenda to show me what I could be. By March, I made a decision that I not only wanted my family back, but I wanted my marriage back as well. I wanted to be a whole person. I quit my weekend job and started staying home.

I soon began seeing the same counselor Glenda had seen during our separation. I told God to either bring healing to my life or take my life. I was so desperate for emotional healing that I even told Him if He did not heal me, I would kill myself and I meant it! It was at that point that I gave God permission to do whatever was necessary to bring healing to my life. I gave Him permission to reveal anything buried in my subconscious to my conscious mind. I told God that I would provide the man, if He would provide the grace, knowledge, wisdom, strength and resources. God honored that request.

God placed me in a position where I had unlimited time to reflect and begin the renewal process in my life. He began to show me why my marriage had failed. I shared these insights with my counselor. He was amazed what God was teaching me. After a few months, the counselor suggested that I needed to share these principles with other couples whose marriages were in trouble. Hence, in May 1988, I began working with couples that he referred to me from the counseling center. This proved to be another one of God's methods of bringing healing to my life and marriage.

This all happened because God did not give up on me and because I had a wife who had the faith to believe God could perform a miracle in our marriage. I would not be in a ministry helping people build strong marriages and families nor writing this book if God had not done such a marvelous work in our lives.

This book is unique because it is deeply personal. It is my story of discovering the areas that were missing in my marriage and family. It is the story of God's grace so I may share the principles I learned with others who are in search of spiritual and emotional healing.

The purpose in writing this book is to point individuals and couples to the Lord Jesus Christ and biblical principles. Under the leadership of the Holy Spirit, I pray that I can teach the basic principles God revealed to me and:

- Marriages and families will become stronger
- Hope will come to marriages and families that are in trouble and possibly on the verge of dissolving.
- Courage will be renewed for those who are separated, but who desire to see their relationship reconciled.
- Christian married couples will be enabled to become mentors for other troubled marriages and families.
- Individuals who are planning to marry will be adequately prepared.

The illustrations in this book are true, only the names were changed to protect individuals who are still in process...and may need more time to heal.

PART ONE:

PRINCIPLES OF MARRIAGE

Chapter 1

Establishing a Common Ground

When I made the commitment to rebuild my marriage, the first thing I did, even before seeing my counselor, was go to the Bible. I opened it to Luke 6:46-49 *"And why do you call Me, 'Lord, Lord,' and do not do what I say? Everyone who comes to Me, and hears My words, and acts upon them, I will show you whom he is like: he is like a man building a house, who dug deep and laid a foundation upon the rock; and when a flood arose, the rivers burst against that house and could not shake it, because it had been well built. But the one who has heard, and has not acted accordingly, is like a man who built a house upon the ground without any foundation; and the river burst against it and immediately it collapsed, and the ruin of that house was great."* I remember praying, "Okay, Lord, what are you trying to tell me?"

In order for any relationship to be fulfilling, one thing that must be present or exist is **common ground**. The Lord taught me this principle very early in my counseling experience, when Vernon and Jennifer came to me for marriage counseling. When I asked them why they came, rather than answering the question, they began to argue and verbally fought each other for the entire fifty-minute session.

At the end of the first session, I told them, "Our time is up, let's pray."

We prayed and they set an appointment for the next week. When they came in for their second appointment, I asked them what issues needed to be discussed. They spent another 50 minutes arguing and verbally attacking each other. I just sat there and listened. I did not know what to do.

Once again, at the end of their session, I ended by saying, "Our time is up, let's pray."

Chapter 1   *Establishing a Common Ground*

As they left my office, I silently prayed they would not schedule another appointment. That prayer went unanswered as they set another appointment for the following week. When I picked up their folder from the secretary the day of their appointment, I panicked! I prayed, "God, you have got to help me. I cannot take another session like the previous two."

The following Tuesday they were my first appointment of the day. When Vernon and Jennifer came in, I asked them, "How was your past week?"

That question was the bell for round three to pick up where they had left off from the previous session. I do not think they had spoken to each other from the last time they had left my office until they came back for this appointment. After a couple of moments, the Holy Spirit revealed to me the principle, **common ground** must be present or existing for any marriage or relationship to be fulfilling.

I remember saying to them, "Wait a minute! This is getting nowhere. May I ask you some questions?"

They said, "yes".

"You checked on the information form they you are both Christians. Is that correct?"

Vernon and Jennifer both agreed.

"It also says you go to church regularly. How regular?"

"Every Sunday morning, Sunday evening and Wednesday night," Vernon answered.

Jennifer added, "We go practically every time the church doors are opened."

"As Christians, do you believe the Bible is the Word of God?"

They both nodded.

"Do you believe the Bible is God's inspired Word?"

They both agreed.

"Do you believe the Bible contains principles for us to live by?"

"Of course", they both said.

"Do you believe the Bible contains principles which are to govern your marriage?"

There was a pause and Vernon replied, "I've never thought about the Bible in those terms."

I asked them, "Are you willing to adopt the principles found in God's Word as the common ground upon which to govern your marriage? Before you

22

answer that question, think about what it means. If you answer yes, you are saying that if you need to break old habits, you will break them. If you need to learn new methods of doing things, you will learn them. If the Bible says you are to do something, you will do it whether you feel like it or not."

There was a silence. Vernon and Jennifer did not say anything for a few moments. They looked around the room, up at the ceiling, at each other and then at me. Then simultaneously, they both answered, "Yes".

They made a commitment to make the Bible the common ground for their marriage and in five weeks, I saw their marriage turn around 180 degrees.

I have found many Christians today are struggling with the same situation as Vernon and Jennifer. We apply Biblical principles in every area of life except our marriages and family relationships. For your marriage, my marriage, any marriage to be successful, there must be common ground.

When you got married, what was the common ground of your marriage? For most people, including Glenda and I, the answer is love. Love is important, but it is not enough. It was not long after Glenda and I married, I began to realize that my definition of love was a lot different from Glenda's definition. This is probably true with most marriages.

What is the common ground of your marital relationship today? If it is not already, I hope by the time you finish reading this book, your answer will be, Christ and biblical principles.

The Holy Spirit taught me in Luke 6:46-49 any marriage or relationship which is not built on Jesus' teachings and the principles found in God's word, will collapse when the storms of life hit. The marriage that is built on the teachings of Jesus and the principles found in God's word, will stand firm, and not waver as the tornadoes or hurricanes come.

January 28, 1986, thousands of people watched the Space Shuttle Challenger lift off from Cape Kennedy. The seven astronauts aboard were highly trained for this mission. Those watching rejoiced in this history-making event. Within a few moments after liftoff, the rejoicing turned to shock and unbelief as they watched The Challenge explode and all seven on board died. What caused that disaster? One conclusion was than an "o-ring" seal failed. Who would have thought that the failure of an o-ring seal would have caused that kind of disaster? Some minor problems, yes, but not an explosion! The scientists and engineers for NASA had a choice to make. They could resign themselves from any further space shuttle flights and concluded that it was just too dangerous and they could not afford to risk any more lives. On the other hand, they could put the future flights on hold until they could find the cause for the disaster, and develop new safety

Chapter 1   Establishing a Common Ground

systems that would prevent that disaster from ever happening again.

That is exactly what they did. Since the disaster of 1986, every exploration trip into space has been successful, even though not perfectly problem free.

When the Challenger lifted off in January 1986, were the scientists and engineers confident that this would be a successful flight? Absolutely! Do you feel, if they had known a problem existed that would cause seven people to die a few moments after lift off, they would have continued with the flight? No way!

Here is the principle: just as scientific laws and principles govern the flights of the space shuttle, Biblical laws and principles govern marriage. Certain scientific laws were broken, causing The Challenger to fail. The same happens in marriage when the laws of marriage set by God are broken, the marriage is destined to fail. If, however, we discover these broken laws and make the necessary corrections, our marriages can get back on the right course and be fulfilling

God warns us in Hosea 4:6, "My people are destroyed for lack of knowledge..." and in continues in verse fourteen, "...so the people without understanding are ruined."

The space community had a tragically failed mission because of their lack of knowledge. That mission was ruined because they did not understand that a defective O-ring could cause a shuttle to explode. The same principle applies to marriage. We can ruin and destroy our marriages without the knowledge and understanding of basic principles. In order to gain knowledge and understand we must turn to our ultimate authority, God's Word.

We are all familiar with a team that has been on a long losing streak, then suddenly starts to win. The media usually asks the coach what steps he took to turn the team around.

He generally says, "We went back to the basics, back to the fundamentals."

Many marriages today need to get back to the basics. That is exactly where they Lord took me to rebuild my life and my marriage – I had to learn the basics of marriage.

Chapter 2

Defining Marriage

In order to go back to the basics and fundamentals of marriage, we must first define marriage. Webster defines marriage as *"the state of being united to a person of the opposite sex . . . the institution whereby men and women are joined in a special kind of social and legal dependence for the purpose of founding and maintaining a family... an intimate or close union."*

The Bible defines marriage in Genesis 2:24 as the union of man and wife joining together as one flesh, and one in body, soul and spirit. *"For this cause a man shall leave his father and his mother, and shall cleave to his wife; and they shall become one flesh."*

Throughout scripture, we see marriage is not a 50-50 proposition. If it is not 50-50, then what is it? Before reading further, write down your answer. In the seminars I conduct, most answer that marriage is a 100 - 100 proposition, or in other words, both husband and wife must give it their all.

This is not correct, either. Marriage is a 100 – 0 proposition. You must give your all, but you cannot control the amount of effort your spouse puts into the marriage. Ephesians supports this principle in 5:25, *"Husbands, love your wives, just as Christ also loved the church and gave Himself up for her."* When Christ went to the cross, He had no guarantees. He went with unconditional love, hoping that all mankind would accept Him as Lord and Savior. Even though he was rejected by the majority, Christ continues to love not only those who accept Him, but those who are lost as well.

The problem with many marriages today is they are one in name only, but fragmented in soul and spirit due to excess baggage one or both spouses bring into their marriage.

We read in Hebrews 13:4, *"Let marriage be held in honor (esteemed worthy,*

Chapter 2 Defining Marriage

precious, of great price, and especially dear) in all things. And thus let the marriage bed be undefiled (kept undishonored); for God will judge and punish the unchaste (all guilty of sexual vice) and adulterous." (AMP) One of the great tragedies of today is society does not honor marriage in the true sense of honor. Webster's dictionary defines honor as *"a good name or public esteem; outward respect or admiration; a person of superior standing or importance; one that is of intrinsic value; high respect, revere."* If we are going to have a strong marriage and family, we must honor them as God's commands in His word. As the Holy Spirit revealed this truth to me, I came to two striking realizations. First, I realized that my wife, Glenda, and I had never really been one in body, soul and spirit, but in name only. Second, even as a minister, I had not honored the marriage and family relationship as God had intended.

Marriage is the first institution established by God. It is a man and woman coming together as one in body, soul, and spirit. It is an unconditional acceptance of our spouse just as Christ unconditionally accepts us. Marriage, I believe, is the greatest institution ordained by God. Through understanding the scriptural definition of marriage, we see that it is a 100 - 0 proposition for both spouses at all times.

PART TWO:

STRUCTURE OF MARRIAGE

Chapter 3

Leadership in Marriage

Ephesians 5:23, *"For the husband is the head of the wife, as Christ also is the head of the church, . . . "*, clearly states the husband is to be the leader in marriage. This verse does not say he is a dictator, nor should he rule by domination. This was, and continues to be, the hardest lesson I have had to learn. A bitter pill for me to swallow was realizing I had never been the leader in my marriage and family God had intended me to be. When you have spent the majority of your life allowing your wife to lead, it is difficult to reverse that role. In the nine plus years of rebuilding my marriage, I have struggled with developing my leadership. I am convinced that the lack of husbands being the leaders in their homes is one of the main reasons our society and nation is almost spiritually bankrupt and why so many families are on the edge of destruction.

Developing the Leader Within You, by John C. Maxwell, has been an invaluable resource as I have learned to be the leader in my home. Every husband and father should read this book for two reasons. First, God has ordained you to be the leader of your home whether you want to admit it or not. Second, as the leader of the home, it is your responsibility to develop the leadership in each of your family members. Those are the facts! The principles in this book revealed to me the areas where I fell short as a husband and father, yet at the same time it revealed the steps I could take to redeem my position as leader not only as a husband and father, but also now as a grandfather.

What does it mean to be a leader? How do you define a leader? Ted Engstrom, in his book, The Making of a Christian Leader, defines a leader as *"one who guides activities of others and who himself acts and performs to bring those activities about. He is capable of performing acts, which will*

Chapter 3   *Leadership in Marriage*

guide a group in achieving objectives. He takes the capacities of vision and faith, has the ability to be concerned and to comprehend, exercises action through effective and personal influence in the direction of an enterprise and the development of the potential into the practical and/or profitable means." That definition reminds me of Proverbs 22:6, *"Train up a child in the way he should go, even when he is old he will not depart from it."* The writer here is talking about leadership.

John Maxwell states that leadership is influence. Every husband, wife, mom, and dad needs to come to grip with the fact we are leaders! A strong and balanced family is the result of solid leadership. God intends the husband to provide this leadership. The absence of leadership is one characteristic of a dysfunctional family. Remember, leadership is influence. I am so thankful that my wife allowed the Holy Spirit to empower her to be a godly influence and provide solid leadership to my daughters while I was separated from them. I am convinced that her leadership and influence resulted in the Holy Spirit putting a hedge of protection around Shannon and Amy.

Watch the families in your church and neighborhood. Who is the leader? Is it the father, the mother, or perhaps the children? In the home where the husband or father is not the leader, there are problems. Out of all the people who know you best, who would they say is the leader in your home?

One of the many principles God revealed to me was, as a husband and father, I was and still am an influence either for good or bad. There is no in between, no middle of the road. This principle is true in your life!

Here is a principle for wives and mothers. You are an influence, either good or bad, in response to your support of the leadership in your home. The manner in which you respond to the leadership of your husband has a great deal to do with the amount of respect your children learn to demonstrate.

Family members are products of the influence provided, positive or negative, which largely shape their life. In *Developing the Leader Within You*, John Maxwell shares the following poem, The Little Chap Who Follows Me, as a great illustration of influence.

The Little Chap Who Follows Me

A careful man I want to be,
A little fellow follows me;
I do not dare to go astray

For fear he'll go the self-same way.
I cannot once escape his eyes.
Whatever he sees me do he tries,
Like ME he says he's going to be--
That little chap who follows me.
I must remember as I go
Through summer suns and winter snows,
I am building for the years to be--
That little chap who follows me.

God revealed to me that I had made the wrong assumption about being the leader in the home. I assume because the Bible said I was to be the leader, the other members in the family would go along because of my God given position and everything would fall into place. Was I mistaken! The principle God taught me was **position is not leadership**. It goes beyond position to developing relationships. If I could go back and start all over, I would spend more time developing a deeper spiritual and emotional relationship with my wife and daughters and more time helping them to discover and develop their gifts and talents. I am very proud of my wife and two daughters. However,I can see if I had been the right kind of leader, their lives could be more productive than they are today. I cannot change the past, but in Christ, I can redeem the future. From this day forward, I can be the leader God requires me to be as a husband, father and grandfather.

Why is it so important for the husband to be the leader in the home? Through recognizing my own failures and working with many troubled marriages God has shown me husbands need to be leaders to teach and develop the following ingredients in each member of their families:

- Integrity
- Willingness to make positive change
- Developing and maintaining a healthy attitude
- Self-discipline

These ingredients are necessary for a strong marriage and family and it is sad to see them evaporating from our society

Chapter 3   *Leadership in Marriage*

Integrity

Webster's defines integrity as *"soundness, adherence to a code of values, utter sincerity, honesty and candor; completeness."* A man of integrity is a man of convictions. He is decisive, solid and stable. You do not have to question where he stands. He is consistent.

In my counseling experience, I have found the common thread of marital problems is the lack of integrity within each marriage. Integrity is not what we do so much as it is **who we are**. Moreover, who we are, in turn, determines what we do. Children learn integrity by the integrity they see in our life.

According to John Maxwell, in *Developing the Leader Within You*, there are seven reasons integrity is vital in a home.

1. Integrity builds trust.
2. Integrity has high influence value.
3. Integrity facilitates high standards.
4. Integrity results in a solid reputation, not just image.
5. Integrity means living it myself before leading others.
6. Integrity helps a leader be credible, not just clever.
7. Integrity is a hard-won achievement.

As I studied the concept of integrity, God brought this question to my mind, "What is more important; integrity in the work place and society, or in the home?"

What would you say is most important? As I reflected back on my past, my integrity as a minister rated much higher than in my family. God revealed a startling truth to me – There is no integrity unless it is in the home. Image is what is present in the work place and in society.

There is a difference between *integrity* and image. *Image* is what people think we are and the way they see us on the surface. It is our reputation. Integrity is whom we are when our job is not on the line and our position in society is not threatened. Our true self is revealed in our family unit and that determines whether integrity is present or absent. In short, integrity is our character.

I did not know this then, but I now know I was more concerned with image than integrity. Hosea 4:6 *"My people are destroyed for lack of knowledge."* .

Reputation is not character. Integrity helps produce a Godly image. I have found that the majority of couples with whom I work are in the dark as to the importance of integrity in the family. God showed me as I developed integrity with my family, my image would take care of itself. Here is the principle: One's integrity in the home should be a higher priority than one's image in the work place or in society.

God also revealed I was inconsistent in many areas in my family life. One characteristic of integrity is consistency. Today more than ever, marriages are falling apart due to inconsistency. As I allowed the Holy Spirit to examine my life during the first seventeen years of my marriage, I came to realize I focused on being clever rather than being credible in the family. This problem surfaces repeatedly in the couples with whom I work. It is my prayer that husbands and fathers who believe as I once believed, will recognize their blindness before it is too late to repair the damaged relationships. Thanks be to God it was not too late for Him to begin a new work in me!

Willingness to Make Positive Change

Making the major changes in my life made it difficult for me to develop into the leader God required me to become. One reason marriages struggle through difficulties is the unwillingness to allow God help them change. Most of us do not like change. Change takes us out of our comfort zone. From the couples I have counseled, I have seen a desire to get out of their misery, but unwillingness to take the necessary steps to change. They have learned how to survive in misery, and in making changes, they are uncertain of the results. Rather than change, they continue to live in misery even when their marriage and family dissolves. I have heard many say, "I tried to change some things, but it didn't help." The reason the "change" did not work was their motive for changing was wrong. The decision to make a change was based on external, not internal reasons. There is a big difference between the two.

When we make a decision based on what a counselor, minister, husband, wife or anyone else says, it is not our decision - It is external. When we ponder or meditate on what is suggested and how it will help us make our way pleasing to God and strengthen our marriage and family relationship, it is our decision – it is internal and we take ownership. Here is the principle: when we take ownership of a change that is based on an internal decision, it then takes on meaning that is missing from external behavior. Internal decisions become a part of our life.

As God began revealing areas in my life that needed to be changed, I went through what the majority goes through - the fear of the unknown. I thought, "What if it doesn't work, what if I fail?"

In becoming the leader in my family, I found, and still find, I must go through uncharted territory. However, I have also discovered what God leads me to do, I can do through Christ who gives me strength. Each of us can become the leader God requires. *"I can do all things through Him* (Christ) *who strengthens me"* (Philippians 4:13). In order for husbands to change into what God requires of us, we must make the decision and take the action to be committed to making the change. The problem is, too many individuals want to talk and dream about a fulfilling marriage and family, but continue in their present pattern of behavior, hoping that all will turn out okay in the end.

Many of the men I work with have difficulty making change because of negative thinking. If you think you can't, you can't; if you think you can, you can. God showed me I would never reach the potential He has for me as a husband, father and grandfather unless I was willing to make changes in my life as He revealed them to me.

Developing and Maintaining A Healthy Attitude

I was reading Romans 12:2; *"And do not be conformed to this world, but be transformed by the renewing of your mind, that you may prove what the will of God is, that which is good and acceptable and perfect."* The Holy Spirit revealed to me my attitude had to be transformed. The Lord revealed my attitude toward life directly influenced my attitude toward my family.

Due to emotional wounds in my life, I had to admit that my attitude was "you owe me". I can look back now and see that I expected my family to give to me and meet my needs without me giving anything to them in return.

I see this same attitude in the couples I counsel. That attitude must die if a husband is going to be a Godly leader in his family. I am convinced that the attitude of the husband or father will either make or break the family. We must accept we choose the kind of attitudes demonstrated in our families.

The Holy Spirit prompted me to paraphrase Scrolls I and II in Og Mandino's book, *The Greatest Salesman in the World*, and read it every day for thirty days.

My paraphrase:

Today I begin a new life in Christ Jesus and I am born anew.

The path I have chosen is laden with opportunity. Failure
no longer will be my payment for struggle. I reject it and
I am prepared for wisdom and principles based on
God's Word, which will guide me out of the shadows into
the sunlight of God's wealth, position and happiness.

Only God's principles endure and these I now possess, for
the laws that will lead me to spiritual maturity are contained
in the words of these principles. What they will teach me
will prevent spiritual failure and gain success.

I must form good habits based on God's Word and become their
slaves. As a child I was a slave to my impulses, but now as an
adult, I am a slave to my habits.

My free will become surrendered to years of accumulated habits
and deeds which imprisons my future.

My actions are motivated and fueled by appetite, passion,
prejudice, greed, love, fear, habit. The worst of these is habit.
If I am going to be a slave to habits, I will be a slave to good habits
based on God's Word. I must, and I will, destroy bad habits and plow
ground prepared for good seed.

My Attitude: I will form good habits based on God's Word and
become their slaves. How will I do this? I will take the principles
I have or will learn from the Bible, and apply them to my
daily life and become their slaves. I will make a promise to
myself that nothing, absolutely nothing, will retard my spiritual growth.

Today I begin a new life in Christ Jesus.

Chapter 3   *Leadership in Marriage*

I will greet this day with the love of Christ in my heart. For this is the greatest secret of success in all ventures. Muscle can split a shield and even destroy life but only the unseen power of Christ's love can open the hearts of men. Until I master this art, I will remain a useless instrument. I will make Christ's love my greatest weapon and no one will be able to defend against its force.

My reasoning they may counter; my speech they may question; my clothes they may disapprove; my face they may reject; yet the love of Christ in me will melt all hearts liken to the sun whose rays soften the coldest clay.

I will greet this day with Christ's love in my heart.

And how will I do this? Henceforth, will I look on all things with the love of Christ and be spiritually refreshed. I will love the sun, for it warms my bones; yet I will love the rain, for it cleanses my spirit. I will love the light, for it shows me the way; yet I will love the darkness, for it shows me the stars. I will welcome happiness, for it enlarges my heart; yet I will endure sadness, for it opens my soul. I will acknowledge rewards for God's glory; yet I will welcome obstacles, for they are my challenge.

I will greet this day with Christ's love in my heart.

And how will I speak? I will praise mine enemies and they will become friends; I will encourage my friends and they will become brothers. Always will I dig for a reason to applaud; never will I scratch for excuses to gossip. When I am tempted to criticize I will bite on my tongue; when I am moved to praise I will shout from the roofs.

Is it not so that the birds, the wind, the sea and all nature speaks with the music of praise for God their creator? Cannot I speak the same music to His children? Henceforth will I remember this secret and it will change my life.

I will greet this day with Christ's love in my heart.

And how will I act? I will love all manners of men for each have qualities to be admired even though they be hidden. With Christ's love I will tear down the walls of hate and suspicion which they have built around their hearts and in its place will I build bridges so Christ's love may enter their souls.

I will love the ambitious, for they can inspire me.

I will love the failures, for they can teach me.

I will love political leaders, for they are but human

I will love the meek, for they are the sons of God.

I will love the rich, for they are yet lonely.

I will love the poor, for they are so many.

I will love the young, for the faith they hold.

I will love the old, for the wisdom they share.

I will greet this day with Christ's love in my heart.

Chapter 3 *Leadership in Marriage*

But how will I react to the actions of others? With the love of Christ. For just as His love is my weapon to open the hearts of men, His love is also my shield to repell the arrows of hate and spears of anger. Adversity and discouragement shall beat against my new shield and become as the softest of rains. My shield will protect me when surrounded by the indifferent and sustain me when I am alone. It will uplift, met in moments of despair, yet it will calm me in times of exultation. It will become stronger and protective with use as I grow in the grace and knowledge of the Lord Jesus Christ daily.

I will greet this day with Christ's love in my heart.

And how will I confront each of whom I meet? In only one way. In silence and to my self I will address him and say I love you with the love of Christ. Though spoken in silence these words will shine in my eyes, unwrinkled my brow, bring a smile to my lips and an echo in my voice; and his heart will be opened. And who is there who will be able to reject me when his heart feels God's love?

I will greet this day with Christ's love in my heart.

And last but not least, I will love myself for who I am in Christ. For when I do, I will zealously inspect all things that enter my body, my mind, my soul, my heart. Never will I overindulge the requests of my flesh, rather I will cherish my body with cleanliness and moderation. Never will I allow my mind to be attracted to evil and despair, rather I will uplift it with the knowledge and wisdom found in God's Word. Never will I allow my soul to become complacent and satisfied, rather I will feed it with meditation of God's Word and prayer. Never will I allow my heart to become small and bitter, rather I will share it and it will grow and touch even the coldest heart.

I will greet this day with Christ's love in my heart.

Henceforth, will I love all mankind. From this moment, all hate is let from my veins for I have no time to hate, only time to love. From this moment, I take the first step required in achieving spiritual maturity. With Christ's love, I will grow daily and bare spiritual fruit. If I have no other qualities I can succeed with the love of Christ alone. Without it I will fail, though I possess all the knowledge and skills of the world.

I will greet this day with the love of Christ in my heart and I am prosperous and successful for God's honor and glory.

By doing this exercise, I was applying Philippians 2:3-5 to my life. *"Do nothing from selfishness or empty conceit, but with humility of mind let each of you regard one another as more important than himself; do not merely look out for your own personal interests, but also for the interests of others. Have this attitude in yourselves which was also in Christ Jesus."*

Self-Discipline

Another change I had to make in my life was self-discipline within my home life. Even though I was self-disciplined in developing my sermons and carrying out my ministry work, I lacked the discipline needed in my home.

Husbands and fathers, practice self-discipline and chances are you will produce a family who practices self-discipline. I saw this happen in my own home. I learned it is one thing to be self-disciplined in my profession, but another in my home.

A marriage can become healthy, or remain dysfunctional, based on the leadership of the husband. Husbands and fathers, I challenge you to give the Holy Spirit permission to:

"Search me (thoroughly), O God, and know my heart. Try me and know my thoughts. See if there is any hurtful or wicked way in me, and lead in the way everlasting." (Psalms 139:23-24 AMP)

Chapter 4

Husbands, Love Your Wife As....

Christ loved the Church

Ephesians 5: 25 *Husbands, love your wives, just as Christ also loved the church and gave Himself up for her."* Another lesson the Holy Spirit taught me was I did not understand the true meaning of love in marriage. As I began to reflect on how Christ loved me, I came to realize that true love is much more than a feeling. I came to realize my definition of love in marriage was totally opposite of God's definition.

Stop reading right now and write out your definition of love as it pertains to your marriage. Do not ask for anyone's opinion or thought. Have your spouse write out their definition. When you have finished, compare your definitions. Completing this exercise is very important to this chapter. I have had couples do this exercise on many occasions and not one couple came up with the same definition. A few were similar but not the exact same definition.

How does society define love in marriage? Tim Kimmel in his book *"Little House on the Freeway"* sums it up in the poem, The Day Our Lives. *WE LIVE THE DAYS OF OUR LIVES, as THE YOUNG AND THE RESTLESS, realizing that we only have ONE LIFE TO LIVE, and AS THE WORLD TURNS we want to search for that GUIDING LIGHT that will keep us from falling in love at a GENERAL HOSPITAL in SANTA BARBARA.*

I realize his poking fun at the "soaps". However, it is not funny. I have found many couples remind me of the soap operas. Love for the vast majority is based on what they read in romance novels, see in the movies, and what they watch on television.

When I asked Glenda to marry me, it was because I loved her. When she responded to my proposal with a "yes", it was because she loved me. The

Chapter 4   *Husbands, Love Your Wife As....*

same is true with you.

However, it was not too long after we were married that we both realized our definitions of *love* were quite different. How do you define love in marriage? To have a successful, fulfilling marriage, it is **crucial** that both spouses have a common definition of love in your marriage. What should our common definition of love in marriage be?

It wasn't long after I joined the counseling program, I told my counselor, "No matter how much I focus on God or experience healing in my life, this marriage is not going to work because I do not feel the love for Glenda the way a husband needs to love his wife."

He responded by asking me if I was willing to love Glenda.

I replied, "Yes, but you do not turn love on and off with a switch."

The counselor responded by asking me, "Blair, will you will to love Glenda?"

I understood that question because I had already learned to act on my will.

I responded, "Yes, I will to love Glenda."

It was there I made the deliberate decision to make a commitment of my will to meet the needs of Glenda and have her best interest at heart, regardless of what I may or may not get in return, and regardless of the cost. That is exactly how Christ loves me. He loves me regardless, unconditionally.

When I arrived home that afternoon and greeted Glenda, I said to her, "Glenda, I will to love you."

That is not the most romantic greeting to give your wife. She responded, "And I love you."

Glenda knew I was dealing with many issues in my life and God enabled her to not only love me, but also accept me unconditionally. I knew it was God's will for our marriage to heal, and if it took saying "I will to love you" every day for the rest of my life, then I would. Daily, for several months, Glenda heard me say, "I will to love you."

I am convinced, in order to have a strong, healthy marriage every husband and wife must define love and make a deliberate decision to make a commitment of the will to meet the needs and have the best interests of their spouse at heart - regardless of what may, or may not, be gained and regardless of the cost. That definition of love is unconditional. Just as Christ loves us unconditionally, we are to love our spouse unconditionally. The only way to live and act out this love is through the power of the Holy Spirit working in and through our lives on a daily basis.

When you adopt this definition of love for your spouse, you let go of your expectations of your spouse and begin to focus on how you can help them reach their potential according to God's will. God taught me that true, genuine love seeks to be a giver, not a taker. The life of Christ on earth focused on what He could give to people, not what He could take from people. God taught me that in my marriage to Glenda, I am to focus on what I can give to her and not what I can take from her.

After making a conscience decision to love Glenda as Christ loved me, I remember questioning, "What if she does not respond in like fashion?"

The Lord then taught me one of most valuable lessons and principles that everyone must learn. I am only responsible for what I can control, and I will answer to Him for my responsibility and for no one else. God also taught me that when I am obedient to Him in my marriage, as well as in all other areas of life, I have made my way pleasing to God and obedience brings joy that nothing can take away. Right now, I challenge you to take a few moments, meditate on this definition, and let the Holy Spirit speak to your heart as to how He would have you better love your spouse.

What does this kind of love in marriage get you? For me it has kept my marriage on solid ground when all the demonic forces of Satan have tried to destroy what God is building. When I adopted this definition of love, it turned my insecurity into security. I found that when I am secure, fear turns to faith. When faith is present, I discovered that the intimidation that was present turned to anticipation, which in turn replaced worry with wisdom. Wisdom in marriage, for me, is focusing on "what can be" rather than "what if".

Am I still telling Glenda daily "I will to love you?" Not hardly. One day, after several months of daily telling her, "I will to love you," I met her for lunch. When I arrived at the cafeteria, she was waiting for me, and when I saw her, the feelings of love entered the top of my head and did not stop until they reach the end of my big toe.

I walked up to her and said, "Honey, I don't have to will to love you anymore, I do love you."

That love continues to grow and deepen as we continue to rebuild our marriage.

Here is the principle: as you act on your will, wait patiently for God to work an act of release of feelings within you. It will happen in God's time!

Chapter 4   Husbands, Love Your Wife As....

You Love Yourself

In Ephesians 5: 28,29,33a we read, *"So husbands ought also to love their own wives as their own bodies. He who loves his own wife loves himself: for no one ever hated his own flesh, but nourishes and cherishes it, just as Christ does the church...Nevertheless let each individual among you also love his own wife even as himself...."*

Paul is telling us in these verses we can only love our wife in proportion to the way we love ourselves. God taught me I am to focus on meeting the needs of my wife in the same manner as I look out for my own interests and needs. Husbands, you are to take care of your wife as you take care of yourself. For some that is bad advice if taken literally. Now as I look back, I can see that I did not like, much less love, myself for who I could be in Christ Jesus. Another principle of life is we cannot consistently function in a manner that is inconsistent with the way we see ourselves. If I am up and down in my life, I will be up and down in my marriage. Through these verses of scripture, God taught me that I did not value my wife because I did not value myself. You cannot value others any higher than the value you hold for yourself. Matthew 22:37-39 *"And He (Jesus) said to him, 'you shall love the Lord your God with all your heart, and with all your soul, and with all your mind. This is the great and foremost commandment. And a second is like it, you shall love your neighbor as yourself.'"*

Husbands, as we nourish our own body and our own needs, we are to nourish our wife. God placed two resources in my hands that have helped me in this area; *His Needs, Her Needs* by Willard F. Harley, Jr. and *The Five Love Languages* by Gary Chapman. These two resources enabled me to identify the basic needs and the primary love language of my wife. I encourage every married couple to read these two books.

Chapter 5

The Principles of Submission and Respect

Ephesians 5: 22,24 teaches, *"Wives, be subject [be submissive and adapt] to your own husbands, as [a service] to the Lord. As the church is subject to Christ, so let wives also be subject in everything to their husbands."* (AMP)

How do we define submit? The dictionary says, *"To commit to the discretion or decision of another or of others; to yield, surrender."*

Is Paul saying a wife does what her husband says, when he says, where he says, regardless of circumstances and without question? Or is he saying a wife jumps when he says jump, asks how high on the way up and gets permission when to come down? Absolutely not!

What then, is Paul teaching us in these verses? The key to the principle of submission is found in Ephesians 5:21, *"and be subject* (submit) *to one another in the fear of Christ."* Go back to Genesis 2:24 which reads, *"For this cause a man shall leave his father and mother, and shall cleave to his wife; and they shall become one flesh."* This verse teaches when a man and woman marry; they begin to function as one in the relationship. Does that mean they have to agree on every decision? Of course, we know the answer is no. What principle takes over when a husband and wife do not agree on an issue?

Doug and Cindy came to see me because they were having a problem as to who should make the decision when they did not agree. I asked them who was the leader in the family. They agreed it was Doug. I then told them that based on leadership, the husband is to make the decision when they cannot agree.

I told Cindy, "The next time the two of you do not agree, submit by saying 'Honey, you make the decision that you feel is in the best interest of the family and is pleasing to God and I will support it.'"

Chapter 5 *The Principles of Submission and Respect*

She responded, "But what if I know he is wrong?"

I told her this gives her the opportunity to demonstrate respect for her husband as the family leader (Ephesians 5: 33b) and if he is wrong, her response enables him to learn to submit to her (Ephesians 5:21). Cindy wanted to know how this could happen when she supported a wrong decision. I then asked Cindy what was usually said at the time Doug made a decision that she disagreed with, in which he was wrong.

Doug answered, "She says something like, 'I told you so', 'you never listen to me anyway', 'when are you ever going to learn', 'if you would listen once in while you wouldn't mess up', or 'you're keeping your mouth shut and not saying a word'."

"Doug, how does that make you feel?"

"Terrible, rotten, like I can't do anything that satisfies her."

I then asked Cindy, "Do you really want Doug to be the spiritual leader in your home?"

She said, "Yes, but he never listens to me or takes my advice."

I told Cindy, the next time Doug made a decision she did not agree with, say to him, "Honey, so what? We made a bad decision. I am proud of the fact that you did what felt was in the best interest of the family and according to God's will. It is not the end of the world. We will learn from our mistake and be a better family because of it. I am proud to have a husband who puts his family interests above his own."

Doug laughed and said, "You have got to be kidding?"

I replied "No".

I asked Doug if Cindy responded this way, would he make the decision when they disagreed.

He replied, "I guess so."

We are told that the subconscious is completely developed in the third trimester of pregnancy. The subconscious stores data. One piece of data that is stored in every male's subconscious is he is to be the leader in the family. One piece of data that is stored in the female's subconscious is when she gets married; the husband is to be the leader in the family. Every wife I have counseled tells me they want their husband to be the spiritual leader in the home and they are frustrated when the husband does not provide spiritual leadership.

Many wives destroy their husband's leadership, and do not realize it, by responding to their husband the way Cindy responded to Doug. Her response to him damaged his God given ego. When a man's ego is damaged, he will back off and not provide the leadership needed in the family. Rather than risking another failure, Doug was at the point of doing nothing.

Cindy made a commitment, with God's help to respond in the future as I suggested. By respecting and supporting Doug's decisions, she then earned his trust, which enabled him not only listen to her more attentively, but also take her advice. By applying this principle, they were both able to apply Ephesians 5:21, *"And be subject* (submit) *to one another in the fear of Christ."*

Sad to say, many of the couples I counsel are not willing to make this positive change.

In Ephesians 5:33b we see the principle of respect being taught, *"...and let the wife see to it that she respect her husband."* Wives, there is dynamic power in that principle. Do not ever underestimate what God can do in your marriage when you apply this principle in your life.

To my knowledge, no one, except Glenda's counselor and maybe her parents, ever heard her say one negative or disrespectful thing about me during our separation. She consistently demonstrated respect for me, which I did not deserve. Her family and friends encouraged her to get a lawyer and protect herself and the children. She refused, trusting God to meet their needs, which He always did, even though at times it was at the last minute. Glenda was encouraged to date other men, but did not because even though separated, she lived as a married woman, standing for her marriage.

The occasion arose where Amy wanted to get her ears pierced.

Glenda told her, "Not until your dad says it is okay."

Amy's response was, "He is not here, what does he care."

Glenda reminded her, "He is still your father."

Through the separation, she displayed respect for me as her husband and the father of her two daughters. **God honored her for applying this principle in her life**

As the Holy Spirit taught me these truths from Ephesians 5:21-33 and I started applying them in my relationship with Glenda, I found her responding in like manner. I saw her not only as a wife and mother but also as my best friend who would stick by me no matter what the circumstances. The results have been the continuing development of a deeper spiritual, emotional and physical intimacy that meets every need in our marriage, through Christ Jesus.

In summary, I am reminded of something I read right after I made the decision to rebuild my marriage that I have never forgotten. I do not remember the source but have never forgotten the message. The message was that love in marriage is...

- The highest level of human friendship
- The ideal of intimacy, mutuality and loyalty
- A love that is centered in your spouse
- Expressed in giving, NOT receiving.

If the Bible gives us the structure of marriage, why are so many Christian marriages in trouble and dissolving? My wife and I were Christians; I was a minister, yet our marriage and family was almost destroyed. I counsel Christian couples every week whose marriages are falling apart. There are several main reasons why Christian marriages are dissolving. In the follow chapters, I share several pieces of baggage that are brought into a marriage, causing it to dissolve.

Troubled marriages affect the church. In Ephesians 5:32 Paul states, *"This mystery is great; but I am speaking with reference to Christ and the church."* According to this scripture, you cannot separate marriage and the Christian life. The same principles that apply to walking with Christ apply to your marriage.

From my observation, having been a pastor for more than seventeen years, I believe struggling marriages can produce struggling churches. I believe the church can be no stronger than the marriages that make up the church. As Christians, if our marriage is not fulfilling, how can our Christian life be fulfilling? Is not our Christian life reflected in our marriage and family relationships? Sure it is! If the Christian life is not fulfilling, how can one's church life be fulfilling? I do not believe it can.

Up until the last couple of years, the vast majority of churches spent very little time developing strong marriage and family relationships. I have been and will continue to pray that every church will have an ongoing ministry to hurting marriages and families.

Chapter 6

Biblical Priorities in Marriage

After the Lord taught me how to structure my marriage, I asked Him, "How do I have a fulfilling marriage that results in a fulfilling walk with Christ?"

His response to me was I must establish and maintain biblical priorities. I came to realize that my priorities determine my life. Your priorities will determine the kind of life you live. Tell me what your priorities are and I can tell you what kind of person you are. What is important to you? I believe a person's personality is molded in the image of his or her behavior.

Before you read any further, stop and write down your priorities in life. List them in order of importance. To fully appreciate this chapter, it is helpful to have your priority list written.

It did not take long in the counseling process for me to see very clearly that my priorities had been wrong in the past. What I came to realize was I had confused my personal relationship with Christ, with my profession as a minister. I focused so much attention on being a minister to the church that I neglected my own spiritual life. God told me clearly that my number one priority must be my commitment to Him through His Son, Jesus.

I cannot emphasize strongly enough that your **first priority** must be your personal relationship with Christ. There is nothing, absolutely nothing, more important than one's personal relationship with Christ. This is a major problem with many of the couples with whom I counsel. If your personal relationship with Christ is not your number one priority, you are giving Satan ground to attack you, your marriage and your family.

I am talking about a personal encounter with Christ. John 1:12 *"But as many as receive Him, to them He gave the right to become children of God, even to those who believe in His name."* Revelation 3:20 *"Behold, I stand at the door and knock; if any one hears My voice and opens the door, I will come in to him, and will dine with him, and he with Me."*

If you are reading this book and have never accepted Jesus Christ as Lord in your life, pray the following prayer aloud from your heart.

"Lord Jesus, I confess all my sins and I repent of all my sins. I believe that you died on the cross in order that my sins can be forgiven. Will you forgive me of my sins? Based on Your Word in I John 1:9 *'If we confess our sins, He is faithful and righteous to forgive us our sins and to cleanse us from all unrighteousness,'* I accept your forgiveness of all my sins. Thank you for forgiving me of all my sins. Right now on this the (day of the week, date and time) I receive you into my heart and life as Lord and Savior. Thank you Lord Jesus for coming into my life. Amen."

What should I be as a committed Christian? Acts 1:8 says *"But you shall receive power when the Holy Spirit has come upon you; and you shall be My witnesses both in Jerusalem, and in all Judea and Samaria, and even to the remotest part of the earth."* Notice the early Christians were to be witnesses first in Jerusalem, which represented their own home. We are to be witnesses for Christ in our home, to our own family. Is this difficult? Yes, because our family sees us as we really are. In order to witness, we must know what we are witnessing. If we are going to be a witness for Christ to our family, we must spend time daily with God. Time spent consciously communing with Him through prayer, meditation, reading the Word and worship.

Mark 1:35 *"And in the early morning, while it was still dark, He (Christ) arose and went out and departed to a lonely place, and was praying there."* If Jesus, God's Son saw the importance of spending time communing with the Father, how much more should we see the importance of daily communication with our Heavenly Father.

Would you have married your spouse if you only averaged 3 minutes a day; 21 minutes a week communicating with them? Probably not, because meaningful relationships cannot be built on just three minutes a day. I am not sure if a meaningful relationship can be built on twenty-one minutes a day. A meaningful relationship can only be established and maintained through communication. No communication, no relationship; no relationship, no marriage. Yet, studies reveal that the average professing Christian spends approximately three minutes a day communicating with Christ! There is no way you can build an intimate relationship with Christ spending a few minutes a day with Him for six days and a couple of hours in church on Sunday. What God taught me is nothing is more important than our personal relationship with Christ. We should have the same desire to spend time with the Lord that we had when we were dating our spouse.

How do we build a personal relationship with God through Christ Jesus? The first step is spending time daily in God's Word not just reading, but also putting the Word into our daily practice. The Bible is God's love letter to us. We get to know Him through His Word. You may be thinking, "Where do I start?" Tim LaHaye in his book How to Study the Bible for Yourself, gives the following system for reading and gaining a working knowledge of the Bible so you can apply its principles in your life. If you have not been reading the Scriptures on a daily basis, here is where the principle of self-discipline must be applied. To establish self-discipline do the following:

- Read when you feel like it, read when you do not.
- Make a commitment to read daily and be committed to your commitment.
- Make no exceptions.
- Set a regular time and place.
- Read with a pencil in your hand. You are alerting your brain that you are looking for something.
- Prayerfully ask God for a principle that you can live by or a promise that you can stand on for the day.

What to Read in The Bible:

In his book, How to Study the Bible for Yourself, Tim LaHaye lists several ways to start reading the Bible. Here are some helpful starting points:

- Read First John every day for seven days.
- Read the Gospel of John twice by reading four chapters a day. You should be able to read it twice within two weeks.
- Read the Gospel of Mark twice by reading four chapters a day. You should be able to read it twice within two weeks.
- Read the short Epistles of Paul; Galatians, Ephesians, Philippians, Colossians, I and II Thessalonians, I and II Timothy, Titus, and Philemon.
- Read the Gospel of Luke, three or four chapters a day.

Chapter 6 *Biblical Priorities in Marriage*

- Read the Book of Acts, three or four chapters a day.
- Read the Book of Romans, three chapters a day.
- Read the entire New Testament twice. It will take 174 days (about six months) by reading three chapters a day.
- Read the wisdom books of the Old Testament; Psalms, Proverbs, Ecclesiastes and Song of Solomon by reading one chapter of Proverbs and two chapters of the other books a day.
- Read the following repeatedly, every day for 30 days:
  - I John
  - Ephesians
  - Philippians
  - Colossians
  - I Thessalonians
  - James
  - Romans 5-8
  - John 14-17
- Get on a schedule that will enable you to read the entire Bible in one year. Many publishers have published Bibles specifically for this purpose.

One thing the Lord has led me to do is read a chapter in Proverbs every day that corresponds to the day of the month. Proverbs is the wisdom book and that reading schedule takes me through Proverbs twelve times a year.

I also read five chapters from Psalms every day. The first chapter is the same as the day of the month and then I add thirty. For example, on the first day of the month I read Psalms 1, 31, 61, 91 and 121. On the second day of the month, I read chapters 2, 32, 62, 92, and 122. The only exception is on the 29th day of the month I read chapters 29, 59, 89, and 149. As you can see, I skipped chapter 119. I read this chapter on the 31st day because it has 176 verses. God has richly blessed me in this practice.

The second step of building a personal relationship with the Lord is prayer. Remember that reading the Bible is God's dialogue with us and praying is our dialogue with God through Christ Jesus. God showed me my relationship with my wife could be no stronger than my relationship with Him. Remember, Paul wrote in Ephesians 5: 32 *"This mystery is great; but*

I am speaking with reference to Christ and the church." To have a strong relationship with my wife, I must communicate with her on a regular basis. To have strong relationship with the Lord, I must communicate with Him on a regular basis. My prayer time is based on the model of the Lord's Prayer as found in Matthew 5:9-13. As you pray, remember that God is truthful, faithful, and consistent.

I. Praise – *"Our Father, Who art in Heaven, Hallowed by Thy Name"*

I address God with honor and respect. I recognize God has a perfect knowledge of Himself and all things, including me. I recognize God can do all things He pleases to do because He is all-powerful. Nothing is too difficult for Him. I thank Him always for being present, maybe in different ways, but always present.

II. Intercession- *"Thy kingdom come, Thy will be done on earth as it is in heaven."*

I pray that His will be done in my life, my family, my job and my ministry. I pray Luke 11:13 daily *"If you then, being evil, know how to give good gifts to your children, how much more shall your heavenly Father give the Holy Spirit to who ask Him?"* I not only ask Him for a fresh anointing of His Spirit daily, but I accept that anointing with thanksgiving. I pray James 1:5 daily, *"But if any of you lacks wisdom, let him ask of God, who gives to all men generously and without reproach, and it will be given to him."* After asking for His wisdom, I accept it with thanksgiving, knowing it will be there as needed. The only way God's will can be done in my life is through His anointing and His wisdom.

Daily, in the name of the Lord Jesus, I put on the full armor of God. I gird my loins with God's truth. I put on His breastplate of righteousness. I shod my feet with the preparation of the gospel of peace. I take the helmet of salvation, and the sword of the Spirit, which is the word of God. I take the shield of faith, which enables me to resist the fiery darts of Satan and his forces. I ask and give the Holy Spirit permission to loose upon me the fruit of the Spirit; love, joy, peace, patience, kindness, goodness, faithfulness, gentleness, and self-control. I pray a daily blessing on my family and that I will be the man, husband, father and grandfather that I need to be today. I also pray:

- "Father, don't let me get angry at anybody today."

Chapter 6 *Biblical Priorities in Marriage*

- "Don't let me get irritated or upset in a wrong spirit today."
- "When asked to do the extra, help me to do it graciously."
- "If I receive an unkind word, help me return love."
- "Lord, help me to be the husband that would exalt You today."
- "Lord, meet my wife's, children's, son-in-law and grandson's needs through me today."

After praying for my family, I pray for:

- My church and all the leadership
- Missionaries
- Government leaders, national and local
- The couples I am counseling

III. Petitions - *"Give us this day our daily bread."*

This is where I talk with the Lord about my needs. Philippians 4:6 says *"Be anxious for nothing, but in everything by prayer and supplication with thanksgiving let your requests be made known to God."* We are to take all of our concerns to God through Christ Jesus. Supplication in this verse means finite detail. In making our requests with supplication, we then give Him thanks for meeting our needs. Philippians 4:19 *"And my God shall supply all your needs according to His riches in glory in Christ Jesus."*

I did not gain a full appreciation of these verses until one day, I went to get my checkbook, which I always keep in my brief case, and it was not there. I recalled the last check I had written was the day before. Our spare bedroom has my computer and a daybed, which I use for a make shift office. I not only remembered writing the check but also the check number and the amount. I search thoroughly for the checkbook and it was not to be found. I moved everything on the day bed; I looked on my desk, in my desk, under the desk, under the bed but no luck. I retraced my previous day's activities, but still no checkbook.

The following day during my prayer time, I prayed, "Lord, please help me find my checkbook. If I do not find it and someone else gets hold of it, they could write checks on my account and I could be in serious financial trouble. So, Lord, I thank you for helping me find my checkbook."

I finished my prayer time and Bible reading, went out, and got the morning newspaper. Coming back into the house, I was prompted by the Holy Spirit to go back to my makeshift office and look again on the daybed for the checkbook. I started moving various items a second time. There was a pile of brochures, which I had previously moved. When I moved them again, you guessed it - I found my checkbook! I said, "Lord, thank you. What lesson are you trying to teach me from this incident?"

The Lord spoke to me and said, "Blair, I am still interested in the finite details of your concerns."

James 4: 2-3 *". . . You do not have because you do not ask. You ask and do not receive, because you ask with wrong motives, so that you may spend it on your pleasures."* As we pray for our needs, we need to keep them in the proper perspective. Verse 2 tells me that Christ is interested in the details of our requests. He is interested in our reasons, as well as motives for the request. The Holy Spirit taught me that nothing is insignificant. What man may call trivial, the Father considers major. The Lord has also taught me to distinguish between my needs and my wants. Remember, we have not because we do not ask or we ask with wrong motives. It is not my will that matters, but God's will.

IV. Confession- *"And forgive us our debts, as we also have forgiven our debtors."*

Here I pray Psalms 139: 22-23 *"Search me, O God, and know my heart; try me and know my anxious thoughts; and see if there be any hurtful way in me, and lead me in the everlasting way."* I meditate on my previous day's activities and give the Holy Spirit permission to reveal where I failed or came up short. This is also a time for repenting as the Holy Spirit convicts me. As I am convicted, I purpose in my heart to make whatever changes are needed. Then I thank the Lord that He is creating within me a clean heart, He is renewing within me a right spirit, and He is conforming me into His image. I thank Him for transforming me by renewing my mind. I am thankful for my failures because they keep me focused on my Heavenly Father. Not only do I learn from my mistakes, but also, as I rise above them, I become stronger in my spiritual walk.

V. Deliverance - *"And do not lead us into temptation, but deliver us from evil."*

This is where I pray for discernment. Satan is pictured in many ways in the Bible. The one characteristic that stands out to me is that he is the angel of light. As an angel of light, he is out to deceive me in any way possible.

Recognizing this, I ask for the gift of discernment so I can distinguish between what is of God and what is of Satan. I have found in rebuilding my marriage, many "good" things come my way and if I am not careful, I can get caught up in them to the point of losing sight of the needs of my family. I pray that the Holy Spirit will give me discernment to distinguish priorities and keep me from the temptation to do the things that seem "good" but the timing is wrong.

V. Thanksgiving - *"Philippians 4:6 "Be anxious for nothing, but in everything by prayer and supplication with thanksgiving let your requests be made known to God."*

I take the time to thank my Heavenly Father for what I believe He is going to do in my life not only for the day, but in the future as well. I thank Him that He *"shall supply all my needs according to His riches in glory in Christ Jesus."* To thank God in advance, for what I believe He is going to do according to His will, is to pray with faith.

VI. Praise - *The Lord's prayer ends with "For Thine is the kingdom, and the power, and the glory, forever, Amen."*

I close my prayer time praising Him. I do this by reading verses of praise from Psalms or by singing (to myself) praise songs. On many occasions I close my prayer with the Doxology, "Praise God from whom all blessing flow; Praise Him, all creatures here below; Praise Him above, ye heavenly host; Praise Father, Son and Holy Ghost. Amen."

Remember that a relationship can only be established and maintained through communication. **A commitment to establishing and maintaining a personal relationship with God through His Son Jesus Christ must be the number one priority in our life!**

The second priority that the Holy Spirit revealed to me was to my family and it begins with my wife. Within my family, Glenda must come first – even before my children. Outside of my relationship with Christ, nothing is now more important than my wife is. As I allowed the Holy Spirit to deal with me in the areas of priorities, I came to realize that Glenda was never second in my life. In fact, she was not even third or fourth. I had to admit that my selfish needs such as golf, softball, television and even the profession of the ministry came before her. I made a commitment to God that outside of Him; I would make Glenda the most important person in my life. With His help,

I would let nothing interfere.

I Corinthians 11:9 *"for indeed man was not created for the woman's sake, but woman for the man's sake."* I believe that God has programmed in the subconscious of every woman that when she marries, she instinctively knows that outside of her husband's relationship with God, nothing is to be more important to him than she is. One of the main reasons a wife complains is when she is out of her rightful position in the husband's life.

I had started working in the counseling center when one day I picked up Glenda for lunch. When she got into the car, I told her I really needed to be preparing for the clients I was going to see later that afternoon. She told me I did not have to go to lunch with her and it would be okay for me to go back to the office. I then told her that having lunch with her was more important than preparing for the clients I was to see. A big smile appeared on her face and we had a delightful lunch. Spending time with my wife was more important than spending that time at work.

From this experience, I learned that much of what Glenda said was okay for me to do, really was not. She agreed to test me and see if I was willing to keep my commitment to her. As I allowed the Holy Spirit to enable me to keep Glenda in her rightful position in my life, I discovered another remarkable truth.

The counseling center hours were Tuesday through Saturday. After getting home one Saturday afternoon, I told Glenda I did not know what I was going to do Monday, since I was caught up with my work at the office. Her suggestion astonished me.

She said, "Why don't you play golf Monday."

I exclaimed "What? Did I understand you to say, play golf?"

She smiled and said, "Yes".

What was so surprising to me is that in the past Glenda did not like me to play golf or play any sports. Why the sudden change in attitude? By placing Glenda in her proper position in my life, golf was no longer a threat to her. **When the husband places his wife above all, except for God, she feels secure and will encourage her husband to be involved in the activities he enjoys.**

The Holy Spirit also impressed on me to give Glenda permission to let me know when I was allowing other activities to come before her and she does. That does not mean that she controls what I do or do not do. She does not. What it simply means is we work together to plan our lives. I am proud to say that my wife is my biggest fan and encourager. By both of us

Chapter 6 Biblical Priorities in Marriage

placing our relationship with God through Christ Jesus as our number one priority, we are able to maintain a healthy balance and continue rebuilding our marriage.

Once I recognized Glenda's rightful position, I was able to become the dad God had called me to be. I was also able to model for my girls the Biblical priorities God intends for us to keep. I have counseled many couples whose marriage was having difficulty due to one spouse placing the interests of the children above the needs of the spouse.

Mark and Becky was one such couple. Mark never knew his father and was raised without a father's influence in his life. When he married and had children, he promised himself that his children would never suffer from a father's neglect. At home, all his time and energy was focused on his children, to the point that his wife was being neglected. I tried to show Mark the needs of his wife were just as important as the needs of his children. The pain of his childhood was so great that he could not make the positive changes needed to save his marriage and family. The result was Becky not only divorced him but she also got custody of the children. Mark lost what he so desperately worked to keep, all because his priorities were out of balance and he refused to acknowledge it.

Children need to see parents demonstrate Godly priorities in the home. Parents, your children will be products of you when they marry and have children, not so much in their actions, but in their attitudes.

Children need to see their parents involved in activities together as a couple as well as together in family activities. Parents, our children need us to place each other in high priority. One way we can accomplish this is by taking overnight trips without them. I know couples that have never left their children for an overnight trip. When children witness their parents not taking time for each other, they are being taught by example when they marry, it is not important to spend quality time with their spouse.

After the children, come the in-laws, other relatives and friends. Many marriages experience difficulty due to the parents not turning loose their son or daughter, or son or daughter not turning loose their parents. *"For this cause a man shall leave his father and mother, and shall cleave to his wife; and the two shall become one flesh."* This verse also applies to the woman.

Marital difficulty is also the result of a spouse placing the needs of single friends above the needs their spouse. The most important friendship is with our spouse, not with the friends we had before marriage.

The Holy Spirit revealed that my third priority is my vocation - God's calling in my life. Regardless of your vocation, it is important to know that is where God has called you. I was working in sales when I came back home January 1988. Having made the decision to rebuild my marriage and family, God led me to another job in order to teach me a valuable lesson in this area of priorities. I was only with this company a brief time when I came to realize, because of the demands the company had put upon me; I could not rebuild my marriage and family and keep this position.

I met with the district manager and told him what I had been through and because I was in the process of rebuilding my marriage and family, I was resigning my position. He tried to talk me out of leaving. He felt I could be a valuable asset to the company. I will never forget the words that came out of his mouth. "I realize a price has to be paid for success. To get in the position I am in now, it cost me my first marriage."

I responded by telling him that I almost lost my marriage once and because God has given me a second chance, I was not going to jeopardize it by staying in this position.

Too many marriages and families are destroyed due to one's profession. *"For what is a man profited if he gains the whole world, and loses or forfeits himself?"* (Luke (9:25). My paraphrase of this verse is, "For what has a husband or wife profited if they gain position, fame, prestige, and financial security and loses or forfeits their marriage and family?" What job, what position, what prestige is more important than your marriage and family? Too many lives are permanently scarred because a job, a position and financial security were more important than the investment in the lives of family members.

The fourth level of priorities that the Holy Spirit showed were all other activities, including church and leisure time. I believe that outside of a husband's relationship to God through Christ Jesus, his wife, children, relatives and then his vocation, the church should be the next highest priority. You may be thinking, "Wait a minute, doesn't my church life come under the priority of my relationship with God?"

The answer is no. We can be involved up to our ears in the church and never have a personal relationship with God. I have counseled ministers who are successful in the church, but are experiencing spiritual bankruptcy in their life and family. I have counseled with couples whose marriage was suffering greatly because one or both were so involved in church work that there was no time for each other or the family. I know of ministers' children today who are not in church, spiritually lost, because their dad had time for everyone else's children but never his own. A close minister friend shared this story from the pulpit. His daughter, age 4, kept asking him for help. He kept telling her to wait; he was busy. Finally, she walked up to him and said,

Chapter 6 *Biblical Priorities in Marriage*

"Reverend Emery, may I have an appointment with you?" He went on to say that incident opened his eyes to make time for his children.

The lesson the Holy Spirit taught me in establishing priorities is there is a huge difference between my personal relationship with God through Christ Jesus and my church life. Every husband and wife should be involved in a church ministry, first, because all have been given spiritual gifts and second, to teach our children the importance of actively serving Christ. I have worked with many couples that were so involved in outside functions that there was no time for family activities.

In order to keep our priorities in proper perspective – to be the husband, wife, or parent God desires us to be - we must focus on God. Ecclesiastes 4: 9-12 *"Two are better than one because they have a good return for their labor. For if either of them falls, the one will lift up his companion. But woe to he one who falls when there is not another to lift him up. Furthermore, if two lie down together they keep warm, but how can one be warm alone? And if one can overpower him who is alone, two can resist him. A cord of three strands is not quickly torn apart."* Take three equal lengths of a cord and join them together to form a triangle. At the top of the triangle is God. The husband is at the bottom left hand corner and the wife is at the bottom right hand corner. The closer the husband and wife get to God, the closer they are getting to each other. Parents are also placed at the bottom left corner, under the husband and the children at the bottom right and corner under the wife. One principle behind these verses is that God loves us through His Son, Jesus and Jesus wants to love us through our spouse and children. That cord of three strands is not easily torn apart.

We must focus on God! If we fail to focus on God, He cannot work through us. We cannot be the spouse and parent that are pleasing to Him.

You cannot directly change your spouse or children. None of us has the ability to meet the needs of our family members, but God can through us. That is why we focus on God. God worked through Glenda to change me. Throughout our separation, she worked on improving her relationship with God. She did not choose to focus on our relationship, by either pleading with me to come back, or dating others to cause jealousy. This also allowed her to continue to refrain from blame when raising our children.

When we focus on our spouse or children and try to change them, they are going to react to us and that hinders the work of God. Matthew 7:3 *"And why do you look at the speck in your brother's (spouse's) eye, but do not notice the log that is in your own eye? Or how can you say to your brother (spouse), 'Let me take the speck out of your eye,' and behold, the log is in your own eye? You hypocrite, first take the log out of your own eye, then you will see clearly*

```
                    GOD
                    /\
                   /  \
                  /"Two\
                 / are  \
                /better  \
               /than one, \
              /because they\
             /have a good reward\
            / for their labor. For\
           / if they fall, one will lift\
          /up his companion. But woe to\
         /him who is alone when he falls,\
        /for he has no one to help him up.\
       /Again, if two lie down together, they\
      /will keep warm; But how can one be warm\
     /alone? Though one may be overpowered  \
    / by another, two can withstand him.      \
   /AND A THREEFOLD CORD IS NOT QUICKLY BROKEN."\
  /                                              \
 /           Ecclesiastes 4:9-12                   \
/_____\
HUSBAND                                          WIFE
```

enough to take the speck out of your brother's (spouse's) eye." When we try to correct our spouse, try to change them but do not take responsibility for our own weaknesses, problems immediately arise. We must focus on God so the Holy Spirit can point out our faults, either directly or through our spouse and take responsibility for making positive changes. We cannot see our faults and what we do not see we do not understand or comprehend.

What is relevant in the marriage is not what I see from myself, but what my wife sees from me. The same is true for her. The only way I can love Glenda as Christ loves me is by keeping my eyes on Him and make Him the number one priority in my life. I cannot expect Glenda to be submissive to me if I am not in a right relationship with God through Christ Jesus.

God showed me when a husband loves his wife as Christ loves the church, she will respond in love to her husband, unless there are unresolved issues and emotional wounds that have not been healed.

PART THREE:

BONDING OF MARRIAGE

Chapter 7

The Characteristics of Bonding

We read in Ephesians 5:31, *"For this cause a man shall leave his father and mother, and shall cleave to his wife; and the two shall become one flesh."*

When I made the decision to rebuild my marriage and family, I asked the Lord to show me why my marriage fell apart. In answering my question, He taught me the principles of bonding, which were missing in my marriage.

Bonding is threefold: spiritual, emotional and physical. By spiritual bonding, I am not talking about a spiritual experience but a common value system. The Holy Spirit revealed to me that outside of our Christian beliefs, other values in Glenda's life and mine were very different. Emotional bonding is identifying with your spouse's feelings and emotions. My wife and I had to confess that we both failed miserably in identifying with each other's feelings and emotions due to the emotional wounds in our lives. Physical bonding occurs when there is sexual intercourse.

When a husband and wife are truly bonded, becoming one in body, soul and spirit, three basic characteristics will be present. Gary Smalley in his book, *For Better Or For Best, Understanding Your Husband*, gives five principles that a wife needs to follow in order to help her husband become more sensitive to her needs. The first principle he listed was, learning to express your feeling through three loving attitudes: warmth, empathy and sincerity. The Holy Spirit taught me when Glenda and I, or any married couple, truly bonded these characteristics would be present for both spouses.

Warmth is accepting your spouse in a friendly way. It means you value your husband or wife enough to give them your time, energy and resources as they share their feelings and concerns. You are interested in their well-being.

65

Chapter 7 *The Characteristics of Bonding*

Empathy is the ability to put yourself in the shoes of your spouse and to look at the situation through their eyes. You are able to identify with their emotions. To develop the characteristic of empathy in your life, you must first develop warmth. All of us act, feel and think. The order in which we do those three things is crucial in the marriage and family relationship. In evaluating my life and in the lives of those I have counseled with, I have found the majority tends to **feel, act and then think**. That is the wrong firing order. The proper firing order is to think, **feel and then act**. That is empathy. Soon after starting the counseling process in my life, I gave the Holy Spirit permission to help me think and feel before I acted or responded in any given situation in my life.

Arriving home from the counseling center one afternoon, I walked into the bedroom and found Glenda lying across the foot of the bed. Before I said a word to her, she blurted out, "This is too good to be true. How do I know this marriage is going to work out? How do I know you aren't going to walk out on me and the girls a third time?"

I had done nothing that that I was aware of to provoke this kind of reaction from her. The first thoughts that came to my mind were, "if that is the way you feel about it, if that's the only encouragement I'm going to get from you, and if that's the way you are going to treat me when I'm trying to rebuild my life and our marriage, I might as well pack my bags and leave."

That is what I thought, but I never said those words to Glenda. The Holy Spirit checked me and I walked to the foot of the bed, sat down beside her, gently rubbed her neck and said "Glenda, it's okay. You have a right to feel that way, because I walked out on you twice. What is to keep you from thinking it will not happen a third time? I can't guarantee you I won't walk out a third time, but I can make this commitment to you: with God's help, grace and strength, I will not walk a third time."

Immediately, Glenda calmed down and there was no more out bursts that evening. Why did Glenda have that outburst for no apparent reason? Here is the principle: We read in I Corinthians 11:9 *"for indeed man was not created for the woman's sake, but woman for the man's sake."* In God's system of priorities, every wife instinctively knows that outside her husband's relationship with God, through Christ Jesus, she is to be the most important person and thing in his life. As a result, she will do or say things to reaffirm that position without realizing what she is doing. That is exactly what Glenda was doing without realizing it. She was testing my commitment to her and to our family. She had the need to be valued and reaffirmed in our relationship. I have found from personal experience and from counseling couples, wives will say and do things, not knowing why. Often a husband's reaction does not recognize her need for warmth and empathy and instead makes statements censoring her behavior. That is not what a wife needs. What the Lord has taught me to do in these situations is to simply reaffirm Glenda and let her know that it is okay to have those feelings. Remember: think, feel and then act. Wives need reassurance. They are God's gift to us! The greatest gift that God has given to me outside of my salvation through Jesus Christ is my wife and children.

Sincerity is consistency. Our spouse should see in us a genuine concern for their well being regardless of the circumstances or situation. In most marriages, when things are going our way, we are able to give to our spouse the support and encouragement they need. However, when things are not going our way, the tendency is to withdraw and react rather than be empathic. In other words, when it is bright and sunny we are right there enjoying all the benefits. When the clouds begin to appear and the storm hits, we run for cover seeking to escape. The attitudes I saw in myself during the first seventeen years of marriage and what I see in the large majority of those I counsel are like the weather, they are constantly changing. The quality of consistency must be present for a marriage to be fulfilling.

These three qualities; warmth, empathy and sincerity are consistently demonstrated in a marriage relationship that is truly bonded. All the couples I have counseled, except a few, had never completely bonded in body, soul and spirit.

Johnny and Vicki attended a business social function. To be social, Johnny took a drink. Vicki became so upset that she came to see me for counseling. Some of the first words she spoke to me were, "I've married an alcoholic. What am I going to do? We've never had a problem in our marriage until now and Johnny can't understand my feelings."

I asked her to clarify her statement. She told me about the incident which occurred at the social function. The truth of the matter was that was the first time in all their years of marriage she had seen him take a drink. Why would one drink cause this kind of reaction? Vicki's father was an alcoholic and she was raised in that type of environment.

When she saw her husband take that drink, all the memories of childhood flooded her mind and she was overwhelmed. I had a session with Johnny and explained Vicki's reactions. His response was one I had not seen previously in any counseling sessions. Most people, when confronted for behavior that offends their spouse, become defensive and try to justify their actions. Johnny never once defended taking the social drink. What Johnny said to me made such an impression that I have never forgotten what he said.

Chapter 7 *The Characteristics of Bonding*

He said, "Blair, had I known, I would never taken that drink. Vicki means too much to me to hurt her like that and it will never happen again."

Johnny could easily have said, "Well, she ought to know that one drink doesn't make one an alcoholic. She knows I do not drink. Besides, this is the only time it is ever happened. What is the big deal? She is just over reacting. She'll get over it."

Rather than being insensitive to Vicki, he demonstrated an empathic and sincere attitude toward her feelings and emotions.

In the third and final session I had with Johnny and Vicki, she showed me a picture of her that was taken just before she married Johnny. Vicki is physically attractive. The Vicki I saw in the picture was obese.

I asked Johnny "what attracted you to the woman in the picture?"

He responded, "I saw in Vicki the qualities and the character I wanted in a wife."

I then asked Vicki what motivated her to loose all that weight. I do not think I'll ever forget her response.

She said, "Blair, for the first time in my life, Johnny made me feel loved and accepted for who I am. He accepted me unconditionally and I had never experienced that before. I have a handsome husband who wanted a fat, ugly girl for his wife and I did not want to be a fat ugly wife. He deserved an attractive wife and that's what motivated me to loose the weight."

That is a picture of a couple bonded spiritually, emotionally and physically.

A lesson the Holy Spirit taught me here was that the way I treat my wife is the way in which she will respond to me. The more I value my wife, the more she will value me. The more I criticize my wife, the more critical she becomes.

The Holy Spirit taught me the principle of bonding from Luke 6: 46-49 *"And why do you call Me, 'Lord, Lord,' and do not do what I say? Everyone who comes to Me, and hears My words, and acts upon them, I will show you whom he is like: he is like a man building a house* (marriage)*, who dug deep and laid a foundation upon the rock; and when a flood arose, the rivers burst against that house* (marriage) *and could not shake it, because it had been well built. But the one who has heard, and has not acted accordingly, is like a man who built a house* (marriage) *upon the ground without any foundation; and the river burst against it and immediately it* (the marriage) *collapsed, and the ruin of that house* (marriage) *was great."* One of the first questions I asked the Lord when I started the counseling process was, "Lord, why was my life, marriage, and family almost destroyed when my life and marriage was founded on you? We had a solid foundation. We lived our lives according to Your Word."

When I met Glenda, I was the pastor of a small rural church. Glenda was a Christian and active in her church. What the Lord revealed to me as my wife and I began rebuilding our marriage is that being a Christian is not the foundation of marriage. Jesus is described in the Bible as the "chief cornerstone." Isaiah 28:16, *"Therefore thus say the Lord God, 'Behold, I am laying in Zion a stone, a tested stone, a costly cornerstone for the foundation, firmly placed.'"* Psalms 118:22, *"The stone which the builders rejected has become the chief cornerstone."* Matthew 21:42, *"Jesus said to them, 'DID YOU NEVER READ IN THE SCRIPTURES, THE STONE WHICH THE BUILDERS REJECTED, THIS BECAME THE CHIEF CORNERSTONE; THIS CAME ABOUT FROM THE LORD AND IT IS MARVELOUS IN OUR EYES?'"* Ephesians 2:20-22, *"having been built upon the foundation of the apostles and prophets, Christ Jesus Himself being the cornerstone, in whom the whole building, being fitted together is growing into a holy temple in the Lord; in whom you also are being built together into a dwelling of God in the Spirit."* Christ (and the principles in God's holy word) is the cornerstone of the marriage, while bonding (which is spiritual, emotional and physical), is the foundation.

A builder dug the footings for a house. He poured concrete in one corner and after letting it set for several days, started putting up the walls. What will to happen to the walls? They are going to collapse. Why? There is no foundation. Just as walls cannot stand without a foundation, neither can a marriage, even when there is a cornerstone. My marriage had the cornerstone, but not the foundation and that is the reason many Christian marriages are dissolving in our present day's society.

As I began to counsel with couples, I discovered that marriage does not *create* problems, but *reveals* problems that were not revealed or solved before marriage. The Holy Spirit revealed to me that I was created to hear truthand I am responsible to be obedient to the truth and allow my pain to be healed through Christ Jesus.

The material presented in the chapters 8 through 13 may open up some emotional wounds that may have never completely healed. The purpose is not to create additional pain, guilt or shame but, that your wounds may be cleansed and healed through the blood of Christ as you allow the Holy Spirit to work in your life. Isaiah 53:5, *"But He was wounded for our transgressions, He was bruised for our guilt and iniquities; the chastisement [needful to obtain] peace and well-being for us was upon Him, and with the stripes [that wounded] Him we are healed and*

Chapter 7 *The Characteristics of Bonding*

made whole." (AMP) **Jesus Christ suffered and died on the cross so that we could receive spiritual and emotional healing in our life - without exception!** In order for that healing to take place, we must take responsibility for our wounds.

Use your imagine with me for a few moments. I am showing a large hunting knife with a blade sharp as a razor. We are facing each other and for some unknown reason, I loose my balance and fall forward. When falling, your natural reaction is to reach out to catch yourself. Before you can get out of the way, the knife I am holding in my hand strikes you in the chest and you suffer a deep gash. The first thing your body is going to do is what? It is going to bleed. Did you ask to be cut by the knife? Of course, the answer is no. Did I intentionally inflect the knife wound? Again, the answer is no. You are the innocent victim of an unintentional act, but your body is still bleeding from the wound. If you take the attitude, "It's not my fault that I'm cut and bleeding. I just a victim of circumstances," we both know with that attitude, you will bleed to death. Who wounded you? I did. Was it intentional? No. Who has to take responsibility for your wound? You do. You have to allow someone to get you to a hospital, give the doctor permission to clean, stitch and bandage the wound. When you leave the hospital, you also have to take responsibility to take care of the wound. If you fail to take care of the wound, it can be come infected. The result of the infection could prove to be fatal, so by recognizing this fact, we are motivated to properly care for our wound. Who wounded you? I did. Who has to take responsibility for your wound? You do.

The large majority of the emotional wounds we have experienced in our lives were unintentional. However, we have to take responsibility for our healing. There are those who would tell us that we are victims and nothing can be done about our circumstances. The majority of the couples I counsel would rather blame someone else for their problems or wounds, and as a result, emotional infection has set in destroying their marriages and families.

Again, one of the purposes of this book is for you to allow the Holy Spirit to reveal any emotional infection in your life, in order to take responsibility for your healing through the Lord Jesus and become a whole and healthy individual.

As I took responsibility for the infected emotional wounds in my life and as I have counseled hundreds of couples, I am convinced that the root cause of all problems is the sin of rejection. Rejection leads to many problems including the following:

- Unresolved issues with parents
- Previous relationships
- Premarital sex
- Sexual abuse or molestation
- Marrying or remarrying in violation of biblical principles
- Emotional and physical abuse

We will discuss each of these issues in detail in following chapters.

Chapter 8

Unresolved Issues with Parents

In the couples that I have counseled with, unresolved issues with parents is a major problem with the vast majority. When I begin to ask about their father or mother, it does not take very long for the emotional pain of the past to surface. I want to point out that very few, if any parents, deliberately set out to emotionally wound and scar their children. Keep in mind Hosea chapter 4, verses 6 and 14, *"My people are destroyed for a lack of knowledge . . . So the people without understanding are ruined."* Our parents were emotionally wounded in one-way or another, and they in turn pass their wounds down to us. The role model to the kind of husband or wife one becomes is their father and mother. Actions may be opposite, but attitudes are the same.

I was raised in a Christian home. My father was a godly man. He attended church regularly and so did the family. We had daily family devotions. Dad was a man who prayed three times a day. I would say that Daniel was one of his biblical heroes. Dad was the most consistent person I have ever known. His word was his bond. What he said, you could count on. However, he was not perfect. He was a strong, authoritarian parent. Due to his parenting style, I suffered emotional wounds in my life that became severely infected, creating problems not only in my life but also in my marriage. For most of my life, I blamed my parents and others for my problems. I felt my problems were not my fault. If they had done things differently, I would not have these problems. Sadly, this attitude is common in our society today, including the couples I counsel. It was not until I came to the point of accepting responsibility for my attitudes and actions that I began to experience emotional healing in my life. When I accepted responsibility, I stopped blaming my parents for the problems that had developed in my

Chapter 8   *Unresolved Issues with Parents*

life. Due to the sin nature we all are born with, the human reaction to emotional wounds is to become resentful leading to bitterness and turning into rebellion preventing healing. I Samuel 15:23 says that "rebellion is as the sin of divination (witchcraft), and insubordination is as iniquity and idolatry." The amazing fact I have discovered, not only from my own life but also from counseling hundreds of couples, is the symptoms of emotionally infected wounds often do not appear until one marries. These symptoms can always be traced back to rejection.

Rejection can be defined as to discard, render useless, worthless, lack of value, unwanted. You may be thinking, "How could a parent deliberately reject their child?" The rejection that is felt is not direct but indirect, inferred through attitudes, words and actions. Proverbs 22:6, *"Train up a child in the way he should go, even when he is old he will not depart from it."* Ephesians 6: 4, *"And, fathers, do not provoke your children to anger; but bring them up in the discipline and instruction of the Lord."* Rejection either direct or inferred provokes anger. This anger often festers as resentment and bitterness, which can lead to rebellion.

Rejection is Revealed in at Least Six Ways.

1. Lack of nurturing during pregnancy. Research has revealed that a child who was nurtured during pregnancy is more secure and stable at the age of five than a child who was not nurtured.

During pregnancy, the expectant mother is strongly advised not to smoke, drink alcoholic beverages or take drugs. Any of these three things mentioned have been proven to affect the physical health of the child. If physical habits affect the physical health of a child, will not the mental attitudes of the mother affect the mental health of the child? I am convinced the answer to that question is yes.

The subconscious of a child is completely developed in the third trimester of pregnancy. That being true, I believe every child born into this world, knows in their in their subconscious if they were accepted or rejected.

2. Over nurturing during early childhood. The wife is pregnant, and the child is not planned. She did not want to get pregnant and resented being pregnant. She does not have an abortion due to her moral values. Rather than a nurturing attitude, the attitude is one of rejection. The child is born and when she holds her child for the first time, feelings of guilt overwhelm her. She thinks, "How could I not have wanted this child?" The result of that guilt and shame can become a subconscious motivation to become an overprotective parent, which is a type of inferred rejection.

3. Lack of a father's involvement in the child's life, even in the teen years. Children crave the attention and value of their father. When a father does not take the time to be involved in their lives, they feel rejected and worthless. Too many fathers give their children everything, except their time, and their time is what is needed the most.

You can be watching a game of television. The camera focuses on a player and invariably that athlete will say "Hi, mom." What about "Hi, dad?" A large percent of people today are being raised without the active and positive influence of their father.

In addition, I am convinced that one of the ways a daughter can be protected from being sexual impure and becoming active sexually is for the father to spend quality time with his daughter(s). Based on what women have told me in counseling, girls who do not feel valued by the most important man in their life will seek this approval from others, often through sex.

You Will If You Love Me

On a Friday afternoon, Mary, a sixteen-year-old, came to see me with her mother, Donna. The father, Jim, was out of town of a business trip and due to the seriousness of Mary's problem urged his wife not to wait until he returned home to seek counseling. Mary had been steadily dating a guy for several months that started putting pressure on her to have sex. Mary felt she really loved this guy but due to her Christian values and the teaching of her parents, she knew that premarital sex was a sin. She confided in her parents, asking for guidance in how to handle this situation. Many parents would have said, "You'll never go out with that scum bag again. We forbid you to ever see him." Mary's parents at first told her to stand up for her convictions. The boy friend continued to increase the pressure, telling her if she really loved him, she would prove it by making love with him. Again, Mary confided in her parents that she was afraid when they went out the coming night, she would give in. Mary's mother called her husband, who in turned urged them to see a counselor immediately. I believe the parents were wise in their approach by not forbidding their daughter to see the boy friend. Too many times, if you tell a teenager they cannot do something, they do it out of spite.

When they had shared the problem with me, I asked Mary, "What has kept you from having sex with your boy friend up to this point?" Her answer amazed me. She said, "If I had sex before marriage it would kill my dad and I don't want to ever do anything to hurt or disgrace my father." Mary not one time mentioned her mother in our conversation. Here was a teenage

Chapter 8   *Unresolved Issues with Parents*

girl with a father who had invested so much time into her that she felt she could tell him anything.

I gave Mary the following advice; "When your boyfriend tells you to prove your love by having sex with him, just tell him if he really loves you, he will not ask you to sin against God, himself, herself or her parents." Say, "If you really love me you will not ask to violate you or myself. If you really love me, you will love and value me for who I am, not based on what I give to you."

At the end of our session, she smiled and said, "Blair, I feel I can now handle the problem."

The following Monday afternoon, Mary called me to tell me about her date the previous Friday night. Again, the boy friend pressured her to have sex. She responded to him the way I suggested. When I asked Mary how he responded, she said he got angry and told her if she wouldn't prove her love to him by making love, he didn't need her kind of love and their relationship was over. I asked Mary what happened next.

She said, "I told him if he couldn't love me for who I am but only for what I gave him, I didn't need that kind of love. Besides he wasn't the only fish in the pond."

Mary felt unconditional acceptance from her father rather than inferred rejection. She did not need to seek love and acceptance elsewhere.

4. Unrealistic expectations resulting in negative messages, wrong life commands or curses, when the expectations are not met. Psychologists tell us by the age of sixteen, we have received 173,000 negative statements, and every one is stored in the subconscious. Negative statements are a form of rejection. On the other hand, only 16,000 positive statements are heard and stored in the subconscious. It takes from 7 to 11 positive statements to override one negative statement.

Parents, be careful not to place to unduly high expectations on your children. Expectations are needed but they also must be attainable. Often parents use their child's school or sports to channel their unrealistic expectations. For example, Billy was in the seventh grade. His father gave him very little time and was a perfectionist. On Billy's first report card, he had all C's. His father looked at the report card and said, "If you apply yourself you could make all B's. Billy worked harder and the next report card had all B's. His father's response was "If you applied yourself, you would be an "A" student. Desiring the approval of his father, he brought home all A's on the next report card. His father's response was, "I know those teachers, they would give anybody an "A". Nothing Billy could do was good enough for his

76

dad. Billy's father without realizing it inferred rejection on Billy.

5. Over protective parents. Shannon, my oldest daughter wanted to try out for the Junior Varsity cheerleaders in the 8th grade. At first I didn't want to let her try out because I felt she didn't have the slightest chance of being selected, and I wanted to protect her from the disappointment of failure. Shannon had never been a cheerleader, never taken dance or gymnastics. The girls she would compete against had been cheerleaders, and taken dance and/or gymnastics. Then I remembered how I felt when I was her age and my father would not allow me try out for the football team, and decided she could make her own choice. Those trying out practiced together several weeks before they were selected. The day before the tryouts when the selections would be made, I picked Shannon up from practice and asked her how she felt about her chances.

She replied, "I don't know."

I said, "Shannon, I'm proud of you for trying out. You have really worked hard and whether or not you are selected, I want you to know I'm really proud of you because I know you gave your best."

When I picked up Shannon the next day from school, I said, "Did you make it?" With a big smile, she said, "Yes. They read out our names over the intercom and my name was announced first."

I told her how proud and happy I was for her. Then I thought, I almost did not let her try out, fearing she could not make it. When Shannon was a sophomore, she was voted the most valuable J.V. Cheerleader and in her senior year, she was chief varsity cheerleader.

6. Lack of or inconsistent discipline is inferred rejection. When boundaries are missing people become confused, bewildered and feel devalued. I have had teenagers ask me why their parents did not love them enough to tell them, "No". Children and teenagers want discipline and clear boundaries. They will never tell their parents that, but it's a fact. When there is a lack of discipline and boundaries, the inferred message is "I don't really care what you do." That is rejection! Games are not played without rules and objectives. Why should we allow our home, school, or work situations to be without these?

How do we find spiritual and emotional healing due to the wounds caused by inferred rejection? One of the first prayers I prayed was Psalms 139:23-24, "Search me, O God, and know my heart; try me and know my anxious thoughts; and see if there be any hurtful way in me, and lead me in the everlasting way." I want to point out that I do not believe in trying to dig up past "garbage" on our own. Doing anything within ourselves can give ground

Chapter 8   *Unresolved Issues with Parents*

to Satan and his forces to attack and defeat us. After praying Psalm 139:22 and 23, I also prayed, "Holy Spirit, in the name of the Lord Jesus Christ, I give you permission to reveal anything buried in my subconscious to my conscious and I will deal with it. I will provide the man if you will provide the grace, resources, and knowledge. My desire is to make my way pleasing to you and to be the man, the husband and father that honors You."

God honored that prayer. That is the prayer I believe must be prayed as we deal with the emotional wounds in our life.

Paul wrote in Romans chapter 12, verses 1and 2, *"I urge you therefore, brethren, by the mercies of God, to present your bodies a living and holy sacrifice, acceptable to God, which is your spiritual service of worship. And do not be conformed to this world, but be transformed by the renewing of your mind, that you may prove what the will of God is, that which is good and acceptable and perfect."* In order to renew our mind, we must allow the Holy Spirit to remove all the excess "baggage" which we have been carrying and allow Him to heal our emotional wounds.

The first step the Holy Spirit led me to take after praying the prayer mentioned above was to deal with unfinished business with my father. He died in April 1987 while I was separated from my family. I pictured my dad sitting in an empty chair across from me. As the Holy Spirit led me, I expressed to him my feelings, hurt and pain I experienced through his past actions. It was an emotionally painful process for me and it took several sessions to complete the process. The last session was one of complete release and freedom. When I had expressed all hurt and pain, I sat silently, weeping, looking at the empty chair. The question that came to my mind was "Son, will you forgive me?"

The tears flowing, I said, "Yes, dad, I forgive you."

Several months later, I visited my father's grave. It was immediately I asked my father to forgive me for hurting him, rebelling against him and not honoring him the way a son should honor his father. What a release came when I felt in my spirit, "Son, I forgive you and I'm proud to call you my son."

When I allowed the Holy Spirit to open that infected emotional wound, clean it out and bring healing, it also gave me the strength and courage to deal with the other infected wounds in my life.

There are two exercises I have clients work through to find healing from rejection. I strongly emphasize they must pray Psalms 139: 23 and 24 *"Search me, O God, and know my heart; try me and know my anxious thoughts; and see if there be any hurtful way in me, and lead me in the everlasting way."*

1. I have them take four sheets of paper and on the first sheet list all the negative messages they received as a child or as a teenager that were spoken to them directly. On the second sheet, they are to list all the negative messages they experienced through various situations. An example would be not being invited to a party, etc. On the third sheet, they are to list all the negative messages they witnessed as they were given to someone else. On the fourth sheet they are to list all the negative messages they intuitively felt, such as:

- Nobody likes me.
- I am just not good enough.
- Nobody loves me.
- Everything is my fault.
- I cannot do anything right.

Remember, the Psalmist said, "Search me O God." There is a difference between looking and searching. How do we know when we have searched? The biblical principle I used to measure the difference between searching and looking is found in Matthew chapter 7, verses 7 and 8, *"Ask, and it shall be given to you; seek, and you shall find; knock, and it shall be opened to you. For everyone who asks receive, and he who seeks finds, and to him who knocks it shall be opened."* Based on these verses, I suggest to my clients they go through these exercises a minimum of three times, but not in one sitting. The only time one needs to go through exercise more than three times is if the Holy Spirit leads you because of issues revealed during the third time of the exercise. This exercise needs to be done over the span of several days in order to allow the Holy Spirit to unlock your subconscious. Why is this necessary? The subconscious can receive messages not to open up. For example, if you were raised in a home where you were not allowed to express your feelings and emotions, what kind of message did the subconscious receive?

The message given to the subconscious was that your feelings are irrelevant. The subconscious is so complex that it is impossible for us to unlock it, but it is not impossible to God. Luke chapter one, verse 37 tells us *"For nothing will be impossible with God."*

Establishing this boundary of going through the exercise a minimum of three times takes all the pressure off the individual and places the responsibility on the Lord. Why three times? Matthew chapter 7, verse 7 tells us, "Ask, and shall be given to you; seek, and you shall find; knock, and it shall be opened to you." Jesus said in Matthew chapter 7, verses 28 through 30, *"Come to Me, all*

Chapter 8   *Unresolved Issues with Parents*

who are weary and heavy laden, and I will give you rest. Take My yoke upon you, and learn of Me, for I am gentle and humble in heart; and you shall find rest for your souls. For My yoke is easy, and My load is light." Peter wrote in his first epistle, chapter 5, verse 7, *"casting all your anxiety upon Him, because He cares for you."* It is not our responsibility to dig up "garbage". It is our responsibility to give the Holy Spirit permission to search our hearts and deal with the issues He reveals to us.

Once they have completed this part of the exercise, I ask them to say aloud each negative message as it was spoken or given to them. Aloud, they are to address the individual who gave them the negative message and give it back to them, with forgiveness. They are to replace the negative message with a positive message.

I applied this principle in my life as follows: "Dad, you gave me the message, 'If you are going to do something, do it right.' Dad, you spoke those words to me after I had tried, but did not perform to your satisfaction. Those words made me feel like I could not do anything right and as a result I chose to develop the attitude, 'why try, it won't be good enough.' Those words led to my decision to become a low achiever. What really hurt was that you followed up those words by saying 'If you want anything done right, you have to do it yourself.' I have carried that negative message practically all my life and I am not carrying it any longer. I realize now that message really was not about me, but about you. You were a perfectionist and the only way anything was good enough for you, was for you to do it. Dad, I do not have to be perfect. The Lord Jesus loves me with all my imperfections and died on the cross so I could be redeemed from my sins and I don't have to be perfect in all that I do, except love Him with all my heart. Therefore, dad, I am giving that negative message back to you and I choose to forgive you. From this moment forward, when I fail, with God's help I will be a better person for what I will learn from my failures and mistakes. Dad, I've come to realize that failure is not final, but a stepping stone to reaching my potential in Christ Jesus."

You will notice that I identified the negative message that inferred rejection, sent it back to the source with forgiveness, gave myself a blessing and established a boundary.

In the process of my spiritual and emotional healing, I gave myself many new positive messages, established boundaries and had my counselor who is also my spiritual father, to place a blessing upon me in lieu of my deceased father. It is so important in dealing with rejection that you have someone "bless" you as you work through this healing process.

2. Another exercise I have clients do in the area of unresolved issues with a parent or parents is to write them a letter and either read it to them or if that isn't possible, read it to a trusted individual such as counselor, minister or a close Christian friend. By reading it to someone, helps bring closure. In doing this exercise, I also have them to follow the same process mentioned in the first exercise.

The main reason we need to allow the Holy Spirit to search our lives in the area of unresolved issues with a parent or parents is that we become bound to what we don't forgive. The Bible tells us that the sins of the fathers will be visited down to the third and fourth generation. One method of sins passing from generation to generation is through unforgiveness. John chapter 20, verse 23, *"[Now having received the Holy Spirit, and being led and directed by Him] if you forgive the sins of anyone,* they are forgiven; if you retain the sins of anyone, they are retained."

Again, I remind you, these exercises are where we allow the Holy Spirit to reveal the areas were our families wounded us. We must forgive them as well as ask for their forgiveness where we sinned against them. Forgiveness not only brings healing, but freedom. Forgiveness will be dealt with in chapter 13.

Chapter 9

Previous Relationships

Jean and I dated steadily in high school. When I graduated and went away to college, it was not long after that I ended the relationship. When she graduated from high school, she came to the same college. In my senior year, we started dating again and I was convinced she would be the woman I would marry. A couple of months before my graduation, she ended the relationship and started dating another guy, whom she married that summer. I was devastated. The rejection I felt was so great that I remember telling myself that I would never allow another woman to hurt me like that again. This life command that I gave myself caused me to put up a protective barrier that kept me from completely giving myself to Glenda as we dated and eventually married. God created us and loves us unconditionally. His Son, Jesus, died on the cross for our sins unconditionally. In the marriage relationship, which God established and ordained, we are to give of ourselves unconditionally to our spouse. When I put up the barrier that I would never allow myself to be hurt again by a woman, I was not only unable to love and accept my wife unconditionally, I was unable to accept her unconditional love and acceptance. For a husband and wife to be truly bonded, there must be unconditional acceptance and the willingness to be vulnerable, along with take the risk of disappointment and hurt. That is how God loves us.

While sharing this in a marriage seminar, a lady walked up, introduced herself as Edna and asked to speak to me during the break. Edna had been married for twenty-four years. She and her husband were Christians when they married yet the marriage still had problems. Edna acknowledged the problems were with her but could not identify them until now. When I shared this concept of being jilted in a previous relationship, she said

Chapter 9 *Previous Relationships*

the Holy Spirit revealed to her that this was the problem. When Edna was seventeen, she was convinced that Bill, who she was dating, was God's choice as her husband. She was a Christian and so was he. However, Bill ended the relationship and ended up marrying another lady. She was so crushed by his rejection she told herself, she would never love another man the way she loved Bill. No man would ever hurt like that again. Edna recognized that she was still bonded emotionally to Bill and asked if this bond could be broken. I asked Edna if she had forgiven Bill for rejecting her and if not was she willing to forgive him. She responded, "No, but now I can and do forgiven him."

I led Edna in the following prayer:

> "In the name of the Lord Jesus Christ, by the finger of the living God, I break and cancel all bonds and bondage between myself and (name of person). In the name of the lord Jesus Christ, by the finger of the living God, I cut off my body, I cut off my soul and I cut off my spirit from (name of person). In the name of the Lord Jesus Christ, I declare that on (day of the week, date and time) I am totally committed by will to my (husband or wife and their name), to be one in body soul and spirit, thus fulfilling God's command ' . . .. And they shall become one flesh.' All this I do in the name and the authority of the Lord Jesus Christ. Thank you Lord Jesus for breaking the bond with (name of person) and making (name of spouse) and me one in body, soul and spirit. Thank you Lord Jesus. Amen."

There was no celebration of emotion. Edna simply thanked me for talking and praying with her. This was the first time I had used this prayer with anyone except for myself. At the close of the evening session, Satan jumped on my back and said, "What are you going to do when that prayer doesn't work with her?" I almost panicked; however, the Holy Spirit spoke to me and said, "Trust me." As people were gathering for the Saturday morning session, Edna came up to me, tears in her eyes and told me that when she got home last night, she felt a freedom in life that had not been there previously and was able to give herself unconditionally to her husband for the first time in twenty-four years of marriage. Again, she said, "Thank you." I told her to thank the Lord, for He was the one who set her free. I was only the instrument.

A relationship being broken up is not the only reason someone can feel jilted. Frank and Marie had been married less than a year when they came in for counseling. This was the second marriage for both and their previous spouses were deceased. Frank declared that he felt their marital problems were due to the fact Marie was stilled bonded to her deceased husband.

Marie said she felt jilted by her former husband for dying on her and leaving her to raise the children. Marie also felt she was being disloyal to her deceased husband by marrying Frank because they met at the funeral home. Coincidentally, Frank and Marie's deceased spouses died on the same day, and had family visitation the same night at the same funeral home and that is were they met for the first time. They started dating nine months later. It took Marie several sessions to be able to come to the point of forgiving her deceased husband, realizing she was not being disloyal and breaking the bond between them. By doing this, she was able to begin to give of her entire self to Frank and overcome the marital problems.

I had Marie to pray the prayer I led Edna in praying. I still use this prayer with clients I counsel with who have been jilted in a previous relationship. If the Holy Spirit has revealed this is an area that needs to be dealt with in your life, I urge you to pray this prayer on faith, not feeling. This prayer is to be prayed aloud because I am convinced that Satan or his demons cannot read your minds. They are limited in their abilities. There is a specific reason why I have individuals document (state the day, date and time) certain prayers I have them pray. When a highway patrol pulls you over, they ask to see two things: driver's license and registration card. The purpose is to make sure you are qualified to drive the car and to establish ownership of the vehicle. By documenting your steps of actions, you are establishing ownership. No one, not even Satan and his evil forces, can take this away from you. Remember, one of Satan's main weapons of warfare is doubt. By documenting you action, you can overcome all doubt that Satan and his demons throw at you.

Chapter 10

Premarital Sex

The material in this chapter, as well as other chapters, may open up some emotional wounds that may have never completely healed. The purpose is not to create additional pain, guilt or shame, but that your wounds may be cleansed and healed through the blood of Christ as you allow the Holy Spirit to work in your life. The material in this chapter may remind you of past wounds that have been healed. If that is the case, first, thank the Lord for your healing and second, resist the temptation Satan may bring your way to doubt your healing.

Eddie and Amanda, a couple in their early twenties and married less than a year, came in for counseling. The first words out of Amanda's mouth were, "Please tell me what what's wrong with me."

I asked her to clarify her statement. Her response was "Eddie can go out and have sex with other women but can't make love to me. What's wrong with me?"

Eddie and Amanda dated four years before marrying. They had sex on a regular basis during the four years they dated and Amanda got pregnant. Three months later, they married. In a matter of a few weeks, Eddie would not make love to his wife, yet at the same time went out and had sex with other women. A couple of months after the baby were born; Amanda confronted her husband as to why he would not make love to her. Eddie had no answers. In a matter of a few weeks, Amanda discovered her husband's sexual flings. Neither understood why he could have sex with other women, but could not make love to his wife.

The second session I had was alone with Eddie. I asked him, "If you could start over in his relationship with Amanda, would you do anything different?"

Chapter 10 *Premarital Sex*

With tears in his eyes, he said, "I would never have had sex with her or anyone else before marriage."

I asked him, "Why?"

He responded, "It was all wrong. Sex messed up her life, all of our lives. I wish we had never had sex until we married."

Then I asked Eddie if he ever told Amanda what he had just said to me. He said, "No".

With all the excess baggage Glenda and I brought into our marriage, I am so thankful that premarital sex was not part of the baggage. However, this is a major problem with many couples I have counseled.

I have yet to counsel an individual, Christian or non-Christian, who did not acknowledge that premarital sex was wrong. We have always been taught that sex is for marriage. In Deuteronomy chapter 22:23-29, *we find the biblical law concerning premarital sex. "If there is a girl who is a virgin engaged to a man, and another man finds her in the city and lies with her, then you shall bring them both out to the gate of that city and you shall stone them to death; the girl, because she did not cry out in the city, and the man, because he has violated his neighbor's wife. Thus, you shall purge the evil from among you. But if in the field the man finds the girl who is engaged, and the man forces her and lies with her, then only the man who lies with her shall die. But you shall do nothing to the girl; there is no sin in the girl worthy of death, for just as man rises against his neighbor and murders him, so is this case. When he found her in the field, the engaged girl cried out, but there was no one to save her. If a man finds a girl who is a virgin, who is not engaged, and seized her and lies with her and they are discovered, then the man who lay with her shall give to the girl's father fifty shekels of silver, and she shall become his wife because he has violated her; he cannot divorce her all his days."*

These verses teach us that if a girl is engaged, and has consented to having sex with another man, they are both stoned to death. If the girl is raped, only the man is stoned to death. If the girl is not engaged, the man has to marry her and under no circumstances ever divorce her.

I have counseled some individuals who have never attended church and had no Bible teaching who recognize that premarital sex is wrong. How can this be? In the third trimester of pregnancy, the subconscious of the fetus if fully developed. The subconscious stores data. One piece of data that is stored is that sex is for marriage, not that sex is wrong or dirty. Individuals I have counseled experienced some type of guilt after their first sexual experience outside of marriage. Why would an individual who has never been taught that premarital sex is wrong feel some kind of guilt after their first sexual experience outside of marriage? The subconscious is like a computer - it stores data. When the wrong data is entered into a computer, it tells you "incorrect data" or "incorrect entry." When an individual takes action that violates the data God has stored in the subconscious, there are feelings of guilt

How does premarital sex affect the marriage relationship? Pre-marital sex prevents a husband and wife from bonding spiritually and emotionally. Shortly after I started working in a counseling center, I attended *"Learning to Live, Learning to Love Seminar"*, led by Paul Hegstrom. He displayed a diagram showing the man as ninety percent sexual and ten percent emotional, whereas the woman is ninety percent emotional and ten percent sexual. He then cited a survey of women who had sex outside of marriage. Eighty seven percent did so, **not** for sex, but to have their emotional needs met, while only thirteen percent did so for sex. I have found in the women I have counseled who had sex outside of marriage that only one did so just for sex. When a husband and wife are truly bonded in marriage, there is a balance between the emotional and sexual side of the husband and wife.

Men are sexual by nature due to the presence of testosterone in their bodies, which gives them their sex drive. A man can meet a woman, be attracted to her and be ready to hop in bed and have sex. A woman can't do that unless she has accepted a life command that the only way she will be accepted and valued by a man is to give of herself sexually (I will give an illustration of this in the chapter on sexual abuse). Based on the women I've counseled, a woman gives herself permission to have sex to get her emotional needs met.

All relationships begin with a physical or emotional attraction. When this attraction leads to a sexual relationship before marriage, the man has conquered the woman and never gets to know her any better. The emotional growth and spiritual/value system never develops to its full potential and in many cases never develops any further after the first sexual experience. The guilt and shame because of sex creates an emotional gap that can cause the man to stop seeing the woman, who in turns questions her value and self-worth, asking "What's wrong with me?"

In those I have counseled with who had premarital sex, they experienced some type of guilt, regardless of how they were brought up. Guilt is a subconscious reaction to the violation. **The subconscious does not know the difference between fantasy and reality; consent or rape.** The subconscious is programmed that sex is for marriage, not that sex is wrong or dirty. When guilt is not dealt with, it turns to shame. Guilt is positive; shame is negative.

Chapter 10 *Premarital Sex*

Guilt acknowledges a wrong committed, asks for forgiveness and purposes with God's help not to make that mistake or commit that sin again. Guilt that is not dealt with turns to shame. Shame says, "I'm no good, I'm not worth anything and the only way I will be valued and accepted is to give in and meet their expectations." To deal with shame, it must be turned back into guilt and handled appropriately.

I turned on the TV one day, and as I was channel surfing, I came across a program where Gerardo was interviewing several teenage girls who were discussing their sexual activity. The one thing they had in common was that each of them had been in relationships that became sexual, and after several sexual experiences, their boy friends stopped seeing them. One girl commented, "My boy friend said he loved me and if I loved him, I would have sex to prove my love. So we had sex, and after a couple of times he didn't see me anymore." The other girls had the same experience. They could not understand why after having sex with their boy friends who said they loved them; the boy broke off the relationship. As I watched these girls and listened to them talk, it was easy to see that they not only questioned their value, and self-worth, but felt betrayed and used.

I have found this to be true with women whom I have counseled. When a relationship they were in was sexual and it ended, they too, question their value and self-worth, especially when the man breaks off the relationship. Shame is why a man can have sex one time or several times with a woman and then never wants to see her again. The reason? Because, to the subconscious, he has raped and abused the girl - even though she consented to have sex with him.

Remember, the subconscious cannot distinguish between rape or consent and fantasy or reality. It does not know the difference. Whether it is rape or consent, the subconscious reacts the same. The conscious emotions may be different. The only way the man can deal with his guilt and shame is to completely avoid the woman.

In Second Samuel chapter 13, we have the tragic story of Amnon and Tamar that illustrates how a man can say he loves a woman, have sex with her and then never want to see her again. Verse one tells us *"that Absalom the son of David had a beautiful sister whose name was Tamar, and Amnon the son of David loved her."* As you read this chapter you will see that Amnon became frustrated because he could not have her sexually. However, he had a friend by the name of Jonadab who gave him a plan whereby he could seduce Tamar. Amnon carried out the plan, pretended to be sick, asked his father to have Tamar come and prepare some food whereby he would feel better. Tamar prepared food for Amnon, who sent everyone out of the house. He had Tamar to take the food into his bedroom. Rather than eating the food he took hold of her and said, *"Come lie with me."* Verse 12 says *"But she answered him, 'No, my brother, do not violate me, for such a thing is not done in Israel; do not do this disgraceful thing."*

Tamar goes on to tell Amnon, all he has to do is ask her father and he will give her to him. Amnon refused to listen and proceeded to force Tamar to have sex with him. Today we call this date rape. After having sex with Tamar notice what verse fifteen says "Then Amnon hated her with a very great hatred; for the hatred with which he hated her was greater than the love with which he had loved her. And Amnon said to her, 'Get up, go away.'" As you continue to read this account, you will see that Tamar refuses to leave. Then Amnon calls his servants and had her thrown out of his presence. When David found out, he was angry, but did not hold Amnon accountable for his actions. Two years go by and then Absolom has Amnon killed. Many women even though they consented to premarital sex, afterwards feel betrayed and used like Tamar.

Shame is the reason why a woman will continue to be sexually active even though she knows it is wrong. She has lost her value and self worth because she feels her acceptance is based conditionally on what she gives rather than who she is. Shame creates a wall or barrier in the relationship, which results in the developing of an emotional and spiritual gap that is not fully revealed until after marriage.

In order to justify their sexual sin, the couple may say, "we love each other." He may even plant the seed that marriage lays in the future. As the emotional gap widens and the shame increases, the sexual relationship may become more dynamic which is a means to fill the void because of the emotional gap that has started developing. This gap will create guilt, shame, loneliness, low self-esteem, fear, distrust, and jealousy, which is a subconscious reaction to premarital sex. The question may come to mind, why? Again, I remind you that the subconscious is programmed by God that sex is for marriage, not that it is wrong or dirty and that the subconscious doesn't distinguish between rape or consent, fantasy or reality. When an individual has been violated or has violated another, the seed has been planted in the subconscious that if he/she allowed me to violate them, what's to keep them from letting another do the same. The result is fear, distrust and jealousy. The root cause of extreme jealousy and possessiveness is that of sexual sin. There is a biblical principle to support this. Notice what is written in Numbers 5:11-15: *"Then the Lord spoke to Moses saying, Speak to the sons of Israel, and say to them, 'If any man's wife goes astray and is unfaithful to him, and a man has intercourse with her and it is hidden*

Chapter 10 Premarital Sex

from the eyes of her husband and she is undetected, although she has defiled herself, and there is no witness against her and she has not been caught in the act, if a spirit of jealousy comes over him and he is jealous of his wife when she has defiled herself, or if a spirit of jealousy comes over him and he is jealous of his wife when she has not defiled herself, the man shall then bring his wife to the priest, and shall bring as an offering for her one-tenth of an ephah of barley meal; he shall not pour oil on it, nor put frankincense on it, for it is a grain offering of jealousy, a grain offering of memorial, a reminder of iniquity."

Verses twenty-nine through thirty says, *"This is the law of jealousy; when a wife, being under the authority of her husband goes astray and defiles herself, or when a spirit of jealousy comes over a man and he is jealous of his wife, he shall then make the woman stand before the Lord, and the priest shall apply all this law to her. Moreover, the man shall be free from guilt, but that woman shall bear her fruit."*

These verses of scripture teach me a principle that I have seen repeatedly with couples I have counseled. A husband or wife knows in their spirit when things are not right in the marriage. They can sense if though they cannot prove it when their spouse is being or been unfaithful, emotionally and/or sexually.

It is amazing how many couples I've counseled who told me that their sex life became less dynamic after marriage or that sex was the only common bond between them. In order for sex in marriage to be dynamic and fulfilling, the emotional and spiritual bonding must be present.

As the emotional and spiritual gap continues to widen in the marriage relationship, the couple decides that what they need is to have a baby. She gets pregnant and things are great until after the child is born and the gap reappears. They may have another child, thinking this will help. It doesn't. In this process, sex which was dynamic, is gradually losing its dynamics and when that happens the husband begins to get frustrated.

A principle that I gained from William Harley in his book His *Needs, Her Needs,* is a wife can function without sex but **NOT** emotional support. The typical husband can function without emotional support but **NOT** without sex.

When a husband and wife are not emotionally bonded and a son comes along, the wife may bond emotionally to the son and get her emotional needs met through him (especially true if she doesn't work). If this happens, the father can resent the relationship between his son and his wife without realizing it. When a daughter comes along, the husband may bond emotionally with his daughter due to the void in his life and the wife can then resent their relationship because the daughter is getting the emotional support from her husband that she should be getting.

Due to this emotional gap in the marriage relationship, they both can very easily become vulnerable to an affair, emotionally or sexually. I have found in my counseling experience that most who have had affairs in marriage had sexual violations before marriage. **How does an affair start?** Those I have counseled with have told me the same story. The husband feels that his wife does not respond to him and that he cannot talk to her anymore. He finds a listening ear from a female co-worker. He begins to share his problems and she listens with a sympathetic, open ear. She in turn discovers that she can open up to him, finding that he is genuinely concerned about her needs and meeting those needs. Their relationship begins to meet the needs that are not being met in their marriage relationship partly because of the emotional and spiritual gap created by sexual sin. As they feed off each other emotionally, the man begins to make sexual advances toward the woman in order to get his sexual needs met. At first she may resist, but as he increases the sexual pressure, she gives in, has sex with him, not for sex, but to continue getting her emotional needs met. The affair may temporarily instead meet their needs, but it causes the marriage gap, or void to grow wider. The cycle starts all over again. There is more guilt, shame, low self-esteem, emotional pain, more violations, guilt shame, etc. This again reinforces the woman's lack of value and self-worth.

I Corinthians 11:9 tells us *"for indeed man was not created for the woman's sake, but woman for the man's sake."* This verse tells me that woman is a gift to man from God and that she is to be accepted and valued unconditionally, just as God accepts and values us unconditionally. In my counseling experience, I have found that a wife has a great need for her husband to reaffirm her periodically. Husband, your wife will test you to see if you love and value her conditionally or unconditionally and not even realize she is doing it. **How?** She will temporarily back off or shut down sexually to make her husband prove that he loves her for who she is and not for what he gets from her. Everything can be going along just fine. The husband starts to make sexual advances, and out of the clear blue she feels bad, has a headache, when only 30 minutes ago she felt fine. What does the husband generally do when his wife denies him sex? He gets upset, angry, pouts, goes and watches television or turns over and goes to sleep. This tells his wife she is not loved for herself, but for what she gives, or for what he can get from her. He is giving her the message, a life command, that his love for her is based conditionally on her performance. Our subconscious is programmed to be loved and valued unconditionally for who we are, not conditionally based on our performance. Because God creates us this way we, especially wives, have a tremendous need for affirmation. One of the ways a wife may seek affirmation that she is unconditionally accepted, is to shut down sexually (a subconscious reaction). After going through this process many times and receiving the same negative reaction, she accepts the life command that she is loved for what she gives and not for whom she is, shuts down emotionally and begins to operate off adrenaline in the marriage. When the adrenaline runs out, the wife walks out of the marriage. I have found that a wife can function in the marriage off adrenaline for a period of seven or more years. One day the adrenaline runs out and when it does, she walks out and the husband says, "I didn't know anything was wrong." The wife in all probability will go through this process if sexual sins have not been committed.

What is the proper response for a husband to make when his wife turned down his sexual advances? He affirms her by saying something like "Honey, it's okay. I love you for you, not just for sex. I just want to hold you and be close to you."

I have had men tell me after taking this approach their sexual intimacy with their wives greatly increased. Why? She felt unconditional love, acceptance and value.

If there has been more than one sexual partner before marriage, will that affect the marriage relationship? What if you and your spouse did not have premarital sex, but there were sexual violations with others, will that affect one's marriage? The answer to both questions is, YES! Look at I Corinthians 6: 13b-18 " . . . . *The body is not intended for sexual immorality but [is intended] for the Lord, and the Lord [is intended] for the body [to save, sanctify, and raise it again]. And God both raised the Lord to life and will raise us up by His power. Do you not see and know that your bodies are members of Christ? Am I therefore to take the parts of Christ and make them parts of a prostitute? Never! Never! Or do you not know and realize that when a man joins himself to a prostitute he becomes one body with her? The two it is written, shall become one flesh. [Genesis 2:24].' But the person who is united to the Lord becomes one spirit with Him. Shun immorality and all sexual looseness [flee from impurity in thought, word, or deed] Any other sin a man commits is one outside the body, but he who commits sexual immorality sins against his own body."* (AMP)

It is important to note forgiveness of sins means that God is not going to hold them against us anymore. It does not mean that there will be no consequences and we will be accepted by society as if nothing ever happened. Galatians 6:7 tells us *"Do not be deceived, God is not mocked; for whatever a man sows, this he will also reap."* Proverbs 6:32 *"The one who commits adultery (any sexual sin) with a woman (anyone) is lacking sense; He who would destroy himself does it. Wounds and disgrace he will find, and his reproach will not be blotted out."* Even though there may be physical and societal consequences, all spiritual and emotional consequences can be healed. Isaiah 53:5 tells us *"But He was wounded for our transgressions, He was bruised for our guilt and iniquities; the chastisement [needful to obtain] peace and well-being for us was upon Him, and with the stripes [that wounded] Him we are healed and made whole."* (AMP) Based on God's Word, the spiritual and emotional consequences of sexual sins can be healed! The vast majorities who have committed sexual sins, I have found, have never been healed of these sins. Forgiven, yes, but a spiritual and emotional healing has not taken place.

Notice verse thirteen *" . . . the body is not meant for sexual immorality, but for the Lord, and the Lord for the body."* Take note that the body consists of three elements, the flesh, soul, and spirit. What are the consequences of sexual sin committed with someone other than your spouse or consequences of sexual sin if you have never been married? Verse 16 tells us *"Do you not know that he who unites himself with a prostitute is one with her in body?) For it is said, "The two will become one flesh."* Genesis 2:24 *"For this cause a man shall leave his father and his mother, and shall cleave to his wife; and they shall become one flesh."* What do you think of when you think of the body? Flesh and blood. The body is a trinity: body, soul and spirit. What causes a man and woman to become one flesh? A minister pronouncing them husband and wife? In the Jewish tradition after the wedding ceremony, the groom after making love with his wife would announce the marriage is now consummated. Intercourse is the only way a man and woman can become one flesh. Verse seventeen *"But he who unites himself with the Lord is one with Him in spirit."* Take note that we are to be one in Christ! In order to be one, we must be one in ourselves. If we are not one in ourselves, we cannot be one in Christ. Verse eighteen *"Flee sexual immorality. All other sins a man commits are outside the body, but he who sins sexually sins against his own body."* We know that alcohol, drug use, etc., are sins against one's physical body. What is Paul talking about here in verse eighteen when he says, "sexual sins are against one's own body?" Remember when we are talking about the body, we are also talking about the soul. WHY? Flesh and blood will not inherit heaven. I Corinthians 15:50 tells us, "...that flesh and blood cannot inherit the kingdom of heaven, nor does the perishable inherit the imperishable." Only the soul and spirit are eternal and will inherit the kingdom of heaven. The flesh and blood will be transformed into a glorified body.

How many can you be one with? Only one. What is the principle/application if there has been more than one sexual partner? The truth I am about to share with you is one of the major reasons I feel second marriages have so many problems. For every person that one has had intercourse with, part of his soul fragmented off to that person and part of that person's soul is fragmented off to them. They are no longer one nor can they be one (unless there is a healing of the soul and spirit, which is discussed later) with Christ. As a result they cannot become one with their spouse. They never bond in marriage.

One questions that I ask many of the couples who have had multiple sex partners is "Have there been times when you said or did things that afterwards you knew or felt it wasn't you?" A high percentage responded with a "yes". Remember, sexual sin is the only sin against your soul and spirit. The reason an individual may say or do things that really isn't them is that part of their soul and spirit is missing due to sexual sin, and the missing part of them is replaced with the fragments of the soul and spirit of the ones with whom they've had sex. I am convinced that different behavior patterns can develop in one's life due to sexual sin.

One of the major causes of personality disorders and multiple personalities is sexual abuse. The subconscious is developed in the third trimester of pregnancy and fully developed at birth. The subconscious stores data. As previously mentioned, one piece of data stored is that sex is for marriage, not that sex is wrong or dirty. That is why a baby can be sexually abused, never recall it, but at the age of puberty, will display the symptoms and act like an abused child. The subconscious knows and reacts accordingly. That is one reason, I have been told, why subliminal messages cannot be used in advertising. Again, that is the reason why everyone I have ever counseled experienced some type of guilt after the first sexual experience outside of marriage. Remember: the subconscious cannot distinguish between fantasy or reality; rape or consent. To the subconscious, any sexual activity outside marriage is rape or abuse. Now I understand why adultery in the Old Testament was punishable by death. Sexual sin fragments one soul and spirit and they are not one!

Another consequence of sexual sin, in many cases, is pregnancy. When pregnancy is involved in the marriage decision, this question will inevitably arise: "Would we have gotten married if there had been no pregnancy?" That question can never be answered. So how do you deal with it so Satan cannot destroy the marriage? First, ask for and forgive each other for your sexual sin. Second, honestly admit you do not know, but you accept each other as God's choice and with His help will have the best marriage and family possible. Then thank God for each other.

How does one receive spiritual and emotional healing from sexual sin? First, ask for and accept God's forgiveness, forgive the ones you had sex with and then forgive yourself. Second, write down the name or place for each sexual sin and pray the following prayer out loud: **"In the name of the Lord Jesus Christ, by the finger of the Living God, I break and cancel all the bonds and bondage between me and [name of individual(s)) or place(s)]. In the name of the Lord Jesus Christ, by the finger of the Living God, I cut off my body and I cut off my soul from [name of individual(s) or place(s)]. Holy Spirit, in the name of the Lord Jesus Christ I ask and give you permission to cut off and send back all the soul fragments of [name of individual(s) or place(s)] from me back to them. Holy Spirit, in the name of the Lord Jesus Christ, I ask you and give you permission to return to me all my soul fragments from [name of individual(s) or place(s)], and to bring total and complete spiritual and emotional healing to my life. This I do in the name and the authority of the Lord Jesus Christ, so that I can be one within myself and then be one in Christ. In the name of the Lord Jesus Christ on (day, date and time), I declare that I am totally committed by will to be one with my (husband or wife and their name) so that we will be one in body and soul thus fulfilling God's command; "The two shall become one flesh." All this I do in the name of the Lord Jesus Christ. Thank you Lord Jesus for making me whole. Amen"**

Before I pray this prayer with the individual, I tell them this is an act of their will to make their way pleasing to God. It is not an emotional experience. I tell them they may feel differently when we finish or they may feel nothing. Every individual's response has been different, but all, found spiritual and emotional healing in their life. The majority finds release immediately, although some did not feel a release until days later. That is the reason for documenting one's action. When Satan and his demons try to get you to doubt what God has done in your life, you can throw it back in his face by telling him not only what you have done, but also when you did it. Freedom comes as we consistently resist Satan.

I have seen behavior change because of allowing the Holy Spirit to bring spiritual and emotional healing, making the individual whole and enabling them to be one in Christ Jesus. This exercise will work only when the Holy Spirit convicts the individual to do it and the motive is to make their way pleasing to God.

You may be thinking, "What if I can't remember all the names or places?"

Chapter 10 *Premarital Sex*

That is not a problem. Pray the following prayer: "Holy Spirit, in the name of the Lord Jesus Christ, to make my way pleasing to my Heavenly Father, I give you permission to give me recall of the name of every person that I committed sexual sin with or the place and thank you for doing so. Amen." For some, all the names came back immediately. For others it took several days before their list was complete. I suggest to those I counsel to carry a small note pad so when the Holy Spirit reveals a name or place, they can immediately write it down. Again, I want to emphasize this exercise will not work unless you are convicted in heart you should do it to make your way pleasing to God.

When a Jewish couple married, a wedding feast lasted from seven to fourteen days. At the conclusion of the wedding feast, the family and guests walked the bride and groom through the streets to the groom's home. The couple went in the house, they made love and the groom would and announce, "the marriage is now consummated." The wedding ceremony does not make the husband and wife become one. The couple becomes one when there is intercourse. When intercourse takes place before marriage, Satan is given all kinds of ground to attack and destroy the marriage through the weapons of guilt, shame, loneliness, low self-esteem, fear distrust and jealousy.

If you have been or are presently involved in premarital sex, I urge you to apply the principles given in this book and allow the Holy Spirit to bring spiritual and emotional healing to your life through Christ Jesus.

Chapter 11

Sexual Abuse

It has only been in the last two decades that sexual abuse has come out of the closet. I have found in the couples that I have worked with that close to 40 % of the females have been sexually abused. I am also convinced that some were sexually abused in childhood, but due to the emotional pain of the abuse, blocked it out of their conscience and have no recall whatsoever of the abuse. However, the signs and symptoms are present.

One reason I believe this due to the fact that I was sexually abused at the age of 11 by an older male. The trauma of that event was so great that I blocked it out of my conscious mind. It was only after I had started working with couples that my abuse came to my conscious mind. Now I understand why I told God when I started my own counseling that if I had blocked out or repressed anything from my conscious thoughts, He had "permission" to bring it to my conscious. When my abuse came to surface, words cannot describe my emotions. The recall of my sexual abuse was like an instant replay of the event in slow motion in descriptive detail. The emotional pain and anger was so intense that I honestly believe in those moments if my molester had been present, I could have murdered him. The next few hours were intense as I cried out to God in emotional pain. How could anyone have committed this terrible crime against an eleven-year-old child? In those few hours of emotional agony, as I poured out my heart to my Lord, the Holy Spirit revealed to me a dynamic principle concerning forgiveness that resulted in a miraculous healing in my life. I will share that principle in chapter 13.

Another fact about sexual abuse or molestation is that many people have a false conception of what constitutes sexual abuse or molestation. A large number of professionals agree that the following constitutes sexual abuse or molestation:

- An adult showing a child his or her genitals.
- An adult asking a child to undress in order to be looked at and/or fondled.
- An adult touching a child's genitals.
- An adult having a child touch his or her genitals.
- Oral or genital contact.
- Forced masturbation.
- Digital penetration of the anus or vagina with another object.
- Anal penetration
- Intercourse
- The use of children for the production of pornographic materials
- Exposing children to movies and/or TV programs that have sexual content.

Victims of sexual abuse will carry many of the symptoms. Some indicators of sexual abuse are:

- A personality change
- An otherwise outgoing child becomes "clingy"
- Changes in toilet training habits
- Signs of being uncomfortable with someone who was formerly trusted
- Withdrawing into self
- A child talks about sex acts without having had prior knowledge (movies, TV)
- Moody, crying excessively
- Changing in eating and sleeping habits
- Behavior problems
- Unusual shyness
- Sudden unfounded fears
- The child has unusual need for reassurance ("You're okay")
- The child shows unnatural interest in own or other's genitals
- Changes in social skills
- Nightmares
- Illness to avoid visiting babysitter, non-custody parent, relative or friends.

Based on notes from a sexual abuse seminar

If you have been a victim of sexual abuse and have never actively dealt with it, I encourage you to seek Christian professional counseling. The emotional surgery may be painful, but the healing results in freedom.

One of the most tragic examples of the effects of sexual abuse on a marriage I ever dealt with was when Jerry and Brenda came to me for counseling. They had been married six months. The problem in their marriage occurred even when another man paid any attention to her. She would end up having sex with him. When asked what motivated her behavior, Brenda felt unable to explain. It took two sessions to get their history. Here is their story in summary: Jerry and Brenda met at a party and had sex. Less than a year later, they married. Sex was a major part of their dating life. Jerry found out after they were married, Brenda was also sexual with other men. Brenda's first sexual experience was at the age of 12 with her father. Brenda told me that one of the first things she remembered being taught by her mother and father was that she was to meet the sexual needs of her father. From the age of twelve to eighteen, her father had sex with her several times a week. I asked her if she ever told anyone of her abuse. She said she told her minister and Sunday school teacher, but they did not believe her. Her father was one of the main leaders in the church and due to his reputation; no one could believe he was capable of such an act.

Brenda had been given the "life command" that her only value was in meeting the sexual needs of her father. This life command took over ever better judgment anytime a man showed her any attention.

I asked Brenda if she remembered the first sexual experience with her father, and if so, what she felt. The memory of that experience was very clear in her mind. She recalled feeling that what was happening just wasn't right, even though she was told for years this was to be her duty for her father.

I have never forgotten the next words Brenda spoke. "I know that having sex outside of my marriage is wrong, but I just can't help myself. You know, it's like I'm responsible to give them sex."

Here is the principle. When we buy into a life command, positive or negative, we take ownership of that command. When we take ownership of a life command, we will act on that command. The sad truth is that many people are not consciously aware of the life command that is driving their negative behavior.

What happen to Jerry and Brenda? I wish I could tell you a miraculous healing took place in their lives and marriage, but I cannot. They failed to show up for their next appointment. I called the phone number they had

Chapter 11 *Sexual Abuse*

given me. It was a non-working number. Jerry and Brenda were careful to cover their tracks. That is why I am confident they are still perpetrating the old life commands.

One of the worst after-effects of sexual abuse is that the victim is often so ashamed of their part in the abuse that they prevent themselves from seeking help. Brenda's experience being dismissed in favor of her abuser's reputation is also very common. Unfortunately, this makes it even harder for victims to receive help. One thing I am sure of is the guilt and shame that an individual carries due to sexual abuse can have severe consequences in a marriage and family relationship.

If you have been a victim of sexual abuse or molestation, I strongly urge you to get Christian professional help. You can find healing and freedom in your life. It is possible. I know, it is possible. It happened to me.

Chapter 12

Reasons for Marrying

"Children, obey your parents in the Lord, for this is right. Honor your father and mother (which is the first commandment with a promise), that is may be well with you, and that you may live long on the earth." Ephesians 6:1-3

Duncan Stanton, marriage therapist, states that in the marriages he has worked with that has failed, 80% never had permission to succeed. That statement tells me that the 80% that failed never had a parental blessing on their marriage.

I can remember vividly telling myself, after hearing Stanton's statement, that when either of my daughters got married, I would not only give them away but I would also give them a parental blessing on behalf of both parents. When my oldest daughter got married, the officiating minister asked, "Who gives the woman to be married to this man?"

I responded, "Her mother and I. Not only do we give Shannon to Michael in marriage, we, their parents, also give our blessings to this marital union. Michael and Shannon we, your parents, give to you the **blessing of faith** to trust in God to give you the kind of marriage you both desire. We give to you the **blessing of integrity** wherein you both will live up to the commitments and standards that will protect your love. Michael and Shannon we, your parents, give to you the **blessing of poise** so that your words and actions will build a lifetime of love and respect. We give to you the **blessing of discipline** wherein each of you will discipline yourselves to think and feel before you act. Michael and Shannon we, your parents, give to you the blessing of courage to take a stand against every force, evil or good, that would try to rise up and rob you of a fulfilling marriage. We give to you the **blessing of endurance** whereby you will always rise

Chapter 12   *Reasons for Marrying*

above all circumstances rather than circumstances rising above you. Finally, Michael and Shannon we, your parents, bless you with the ability to trust in the Lord with **all your hearts** and not to lean on your own understanding, to acknowledge God in all that you do and God will bless you and direct your lives and marriage. These blessings we, your parents, give to you in the Name of the Father, and of the Son and of the Holy Spirit. Amen."

With my hand on Shannon and Michael's hands, I cannot describe what I sensed passed between us as I gave them a marital blessing.

The importance of a parental blessing when marrying became more evident to me when Allen and Martha came in for counseling. Here was a couple that constantly argued and fought over practically everything without understanding why. It had gotten to the point they were going to separate and divorce if this problem was not solved. What was so unique about Allen and Martha was they were both Christians and were raised in a Christian home. The had excellent role models in both of their parents. Daily, they read the Bible and prayed together. There was no premarital sex in either's history. We could not bind any access baggage that either brought into the marriage.

Near the end of our session, I asked them if their parents placed a blessing on their marriage. Allen responded, "It's interesting that you ask that question. My parents did but Martha's parents did not approve of us marrying."

Trying to discover the cause of this disapproval, I asked Allen "Did they not like or approve of you?"

He replied, "No. They felt we should wait awhile longer before marrying."

I read to them Ephesians 6: 1-3 *"Children, obey your parents in the Lord, for this is right. Honor your father and mother (which is the first commandment with a promise), that is may be well with you, and that you may live long on the earth."* Then, I asked them two questions. The first question was "Did you honor Martha's parents when you married against their wishes?"

There answer was "No."

The second question was "Have things gone well with you in your marriage?"

Again, their answer was "No."

They both came to realize they had violated a biblical principle, thus sinning against God, by marrying without the blessing of Martha's parents.

I then challenged them to prayerfully consider taking two steps of action. The first step would be going to Martha's parents and acknowledging that God had convicted them of how wrong they were in marrying without their blessing and as a result, their marriage was in serious trouble. I went on to tell them if the Holy Spirit led them to do this, then they were to ask her parents, "Will you forgive us for marrying without your blessing?"

The second action step would be to say to Martha's parents "Since were are now married and desire to have a marriage that is pleasing to God, would you bless our marriage so that our marriage will bring honor and glory to God?"

They both agreed to pray about these steps of action and follow the leading of the Holy Spirit.

Two weeks later Allen and Martha came in for a follow up appointment. The first words Allen said to me were, "Blair, we started to call and cancel our appointment because we don't need you anymore. However, we want to come in and personally tell you what has transpired in our marriage since we saw you two weeks ago."

With a big smile I responded, "What do you mean you don't need me anymore?"

Allen responded, "We went home two weeks ago and for several days we prayed about the two steps of action you suggested. We both felt convicted in our hearts that we should take these steps of action. We called and asked if we could come over and discuss a very important issue with them. They said, 'sure come on over.' Upon arriving in their home, we shared how God had convicted us of how wrong we were in marring against their wishes. Would they forgive us and place a blessing on our marriage because things have not gone will in the marriage? They not only forgave us, but Martha's dad prayed a blessing on our marriage. Blair, since that time, the arguing and fight has stopped. That does not mean we have not had disagreements, but the attacks have ceased. We have enjoyed peace in our marriage for the first time in along time and we wanted to say thank you to you face to face."

"I don't get the credit, God deserves all the credit, I was only His instrument to share with you His truth," I told Allen and Martha.

I have worked with many couples that were having difficulty in their marriage due to bad in-law relationships. In premarital counseling, I always ask how the parents feel about the marriage. I am now asking the parents to get involved in the premarital counseling by giving the couple I am counseling and the parents the **DISC** personality profile. Involving the whole family before the marriage seems to create a unity that otherwise could be missing.

I have also worked with many couples who were experiencing marital problems due to remarrying in violation of biblical principles. I realize that some of you reading this book have a conviction that there are no biblical principles that support remarrying after a divorce. If that is the case, do not ever back away from your God given conviction. My purpose here is not to defend remarrying after divorce but to share how God has led me to work with couples that fall into this category.

Steve and Betty are good examples. Both were Christians, seeking to serve the Lord. However, they had serious doubts if they should have remarried. The reason for both of their divorces would meet the standards of those who believe there are biblical principles to support remarrying after divorce. They asked me if I felt they were right in remarrying. I responded that it was not relevant what I thought, but what God thought. I asked them what they felt God thought about them remarrying. They said in praying and searching the scripture, they only felt confusion. "Who is the author of confusion, God or Satan?" I asked. They responded "Satan." I then ask them, "Who is the author of peace, God or Satan? They responded "God."

For clarification I asked, "Are you experiencing peace or confusion?" They responded, "Confusion." I questioned them, "Based on what you just told me, what do you feel God's thoughts are concerning you remarrying?" They responded, "God wasn't pleased. What do we do now? Do we divorce again?" I said, "No."

I shared with them some scriptures relating to divorce (Matthew 5:32; 19: 9; I Corinthians 7:12-16) and explained that divorce and remarrying was not the unpardonable sin. That what they should do based on their feeling God wasn't pleased with them remarrying, to confess remarrying as sin, repent of the sin, ask for God's forgiveness of their sin and accept His forgiveness. Not only did Steve and Betty repent and ask for forgiveness, but they promised God if others tried to use them as an example to justify divorce and remarriage they would share the difficulties they had experienced by remarrying and discourage people from making the mistake they made.

Remember this principle: You cannot deliberately sin against God and say, "I'll ask for forgiveness and everything will be okay." God will forgive, but the consequences will not be removed. "Do not be deceived, God is not mocked; for whatever a man sows, this he will also reap." Galatians 6:7.

How well do I know this truth!

Chapter 13

Abortion

When Linda came into my office, I immediately noticed from her body language that she was a deeply distressed woman. She began to tell all the problems she was experiencing in her life and marriage and out of nowhere she said, "If I had not killed my baby, I would not be in the condition I'm in today."

Not letting my surprise show, I asked her "What do you mean if I had never killed my baby?"

Linda then told me of the abortion she had several years before she married. The guilt and shame she was carrying due to the abortion was at the point of destroying her marriage. Linda went on to describe how she had prayed and prayed but the guilt would not go way. She had been involved in support groups, 12 step programs and even counseling but still found no relief from her guilt. When I asked for her reason for coming to see me, she replied, "You are my last hope. Can you help me?"

One principle the Lord taught me early in counseling with people was to be completely honest with them and not try to bluff them when I did not have answer. I told Linda I did not have an answer to her dilemma, but I knew someone who did and that I felt I would have an answer for her next week.

After meeting with Linda, I spoke with a colleague and ask her if she had ever worked with women who had abortions. She said, "No." I told Linda's story and ask if she had any suggestions. She gave me a book by written by Susan Stanford (now out of print) "Will I Cry Tomorrow." This book was the story of how Susan Stanford found spiritual and emotional healing of having an abortion. Reading that book led me to take Linda through a series of steps that resulted in freeing her from the guilt and shame of her abortion.

I will never forget the presence of the Lord in that session. We wept

Chapter 13 *Abortion*

together in the freedom she found that day. That freedom was the beginning of building a new relationship with her husband.

Since that time, the Lord has given me several opportunities to walk other women through these same steps and they too found healing. If you are carrying the guilt and shame of having an abortion or know of a person who is, there is complete healing in the Lord Jesus Christ.

The following steps are the ones I have used with women in dealing with the issue of an abortion:

1. Have you asked the Lord Jesus to forgive you of your sins? If not, pray the following prayer: "Lord Jesus, I confess all my sins and I repent of all my sins. I don't want to do them anymore. I believe that you died on the cross and arose from the dead in order that my sins can be forgiven. Will you forgive me of my sins? Based on your Word in I John 1:9 where you said, 'If I confess my sins you will be faithful and just to forgive me of my sins,' I accept Your forgiveness of all my sins. Thank you for forgiving me of all my sins. Right now on this (day, date, year and time) I receive you into my heart and life as Lord and Savior. Thank you Lord Jesus, for coming into my life. Amen."

2. Have you forgiven yourself? If not, pray the following prayer: "Based on the fact that I asked the Lord Jesus to forgive me of my sins, including my abortion (and He did), and I accepted his forgiveness, I now choose by my will to forgive myself for having an abortion. Not only do I forgive myself, but also I accept my forgiveness on this (day, date, year and time)."

3. Tell me about the abortion. What made you decide to have an abortion?

Write out your answer.

4. How do you view God?

Do you know He is loving and desires for you to be forgiven and healed?

5. Do you desire for the Lord Jesus to heal you of the abortion?

(If tears come, let the them flow.)

6. Let's pray: "Heavenly Father, we thank You for Your promise that when two or more are gathered in Your name, You are in our midst. We thank You for Your presence here with us, and we ask You to be our guide as we journey toward healing for (client). In the name of the Lord Jesus, I bind Satan and all his forces that would try to distract or take us off course from the healing we are seeking. Lord Jesus, I know You to be the one true Healer from whom all total healing comes, whether though medicine, psychology or divine healing. We thank You for the healing You are already doing, and that which You will continue to with (client). Guide us now, Holy Spirit, so that (client) will receive total forgiveness and healing from her abortion. May all the glory be Yours. Amen."

7. The healing process.

Get comfortable, close your eyes and relax, so that the details of your memory can unfold. Now (client), I would like for you to let yourself journey back into your memory to the time of your abortion experience. Let the Holy Spirit help you.

Can you see where the abortion took place?

What kind of day was it?

What were you wearing?

What were your feelings then?

Can you tell what has come to your mind at this point?

Allow yourself to get in touch with the feelings that were present at that time.

Now (client), in your memory, I would like for you to look up from wherever you are sitting or lying and look over to the nearest doorway. I would like you to see, standing at that door, what you would imagine a loving, forgiving, and healing Lord Jesus would look like. He may be tall, short, may have a beard, but I want you to imagine Him as you think Jesus would look. He is probably wearing a long white robe and you notice hat He has a very loving smile on His face. He seems to be radiating a deep warmth and love and there appears to be no judgment or scorn on His face.

Then you notice, as you see Him standing there, that He is holding something in His arms. It is something wrapped in a blanket and after a moment or two you realize that He is holding a little baby. He is holding your baby, (client), and He loves it just as much as you would if that baby were right here on earth with you. Now I want you to get up in your memory and go across the room and face Jesus where He is sanding. You look straight at him and He holds your gaze with his forgiving eyes. You realize that Jesus is not condemning you. He is only loving you. His death on the cross and His resurrection from the dead was to atone for all of our sins, so He stands there offering you forgiveness and love. The gentle smile on His face never leaves. You begin to feel His permeating love flowing deep into your heart and mind. I want you now just to drink in His love and allow it to come inside your whole being.

I am going to be quiet for a few minutes, and I want you to talk with the Lord Jesus in silence. Give Him all your pain. Tell Him about all your feelings and emotions that you have, every single one of them. Lay all your hurt and sadness at His feet, give him every feeling that is present. When you finish talking to Him, I want you to be quiet in your mind because Jesus has some things He wants to say to you and I want you to listen to Him. He may say only a word or two or several sentences. You will come to realize His words are full of healing power. They are His healing touch to you. As

Chapter 13 *Abortion*

you talk to the Lord Jesus, I will be praying silently holding you up to our Heavenly Father (give the client several minutes.)

"Are you able to share what your conversation was with Jesus? (Write down or record what the client says and give her a copy and have her read it or listen to it for several weeks.)

8. Committing the baby to God.

I then lead out loud with this prayer: "Lord Jesus, we know that (client) baby is with You now in heaven. (Client) can see her baby being held in Your arms. Lord, we thank You for the love You have for this child and for how You love each of us individually on this earth. Thank You also Lord, for all those children who never make it to his earth, as a result of a miscarriage or an abortion. We know, Lord, that you love every soul that is created. We want now, Lord to commit this baby of (client) to You forever. (Here I ask the client if she has any sense of what the sex of the child might be and if she has any hint of a name for he baby.)

Heavenly Father, it is in the name of the Lord Jesus, we come to You at this point in our journey and we wish to dedicate this child to You for all eternity. We know Lord, that you love this child more than any earthly parent can comprehend. But (client), as the earthly parent, wishes now to commit (baby's name if the client has thought of one) to You, Heavenly Father, to be with you in heaven and loved by You, Thank you, Father, for the love you have for this child. Thank you Father, that one day the souls of (client) and her baby will be reunited in heaven and we look forward to that day. We praise You, Father, and we thank You for all the healing that you are doing at this very moment." (Here I ask the client if she wants to add anything to the prayer, out loud or silently and pause for a few moments.)

"Lord Jesus, we praise You and we thank You for all that You have just done to heal (client) of her abortion. We thank You for (client's baby), We thank You for the new freedom (client) feels. Father, I ask You to continue her healing. Help her to continue to see the power of Your love and your healing forgiveness. We praise You, in Jesus' name. Amen."

(Adapted from the book "Will I Cry Tomorrow" by Susan Stanford)

We all have been emotionally wounded in our lives. It is not so much the wounds that destroy lives, marriages and families, but the lack of knowledge in how we were wounded and knowing the steps to take in how to receive healing for those wounds. Pray the prayer the Psalmist prayed, "Search me, O God, and know my heart, try me and know my anxious thoughts and see if there is any hurtful, wicked or evil way in me and lead me to the everlasting way." I believe with all my heart if you pray that prayer sincerely, God will reveal the areas in your life that need healing.

PART FOUR:

SPIRITUAL AND EMOTIONAL HEALING

Chapter 14

Restoring One's Value

> *"If therefore you are presenting your offering (gift) at the altar, and there remember that your brother has something against, leave your offering (gift) there before the altar, and go your way, first be reconciled to your brother, and then come and present your offering (gift)."*
>
> Matthew 5:23-24

The writer here is talking about making restitution. A paraphrase of these verse could read as follows: *"If you are in prayer and remember that you have offended your spouse or children or have violated biblical principles in relation to your spouse or children, be obedient to God and go to your spouse or children and acknowledge your wrong, asking for forgiveness."*

Imagine for a moment that you own a retail business. I come into your business and shoplift an item from your store. You know I stole the item but cannot prove it and I know that you know I took it but also that you have no proof. Each time I come into your business in the future, I see you watching me like a hawk.

One day a friend of your comes into your business and says, "Did you hear what happened to Blair Slaughter?"

You may think, "Did he get caught stealing?"

You respond, "No. What did he do?"

Your friend responds, "He got saved." What will go through your mind if I really was saved? I will come back and make restitution for the item I stole.

If I fail to make restitution, you will have no confidence in my salvation experience and my witness will be worthless.

The principle I am driving at is that many marriage and family relationships are experiencing difficulty because value has been stolen and there has never been any spiritual or emotional restitution.

How is one robbed of his or her value? There are several ways. One way is through inferred rejection given to us by parents, siblings, and teachers. Refer back to chapter 6 for more information on rejection. A second way value is robbed from an individual is through premarital sex, sexual abuse or molestation and physical and emotional abuse.

When individuals takes responsibility for the spiritual and emotional wounds they inflict on their spouse and/or children, it is amazing what I see transpire in their relationships.

How do we restore value to our spouse and/or children? The following steps are the ones I used in restoring value to my wife and daughters. I have also taught these steps to those couples with whom I have consulted and counseled.

Step 1: Give the Holy Spirit permission to reveal the areas you need to take responsibility. To demonstrate you have given the Holy Spirit permission, write down on a sheet of paper the ways your spouse and children would say you offended them. The one area that many individuals neglect or forget to take responsibility for is in the area of premarital sex.

Step 2: Relive your offenses through the feelings of your spouse and children. I am convinced that true repentance comes only as we "feel" our offenses through the eyes and emotions of our spouse and children.

As I relived what I put my wife and daughters through, and put myself in their shoes, it was then that I was able to understand and communicate the hurt and pain I inflicted on my wife and daughters. This step made repentance come much easier which led me to the next step.

Step 3: Humble yourself in genuine repentance. Going through this step, the Holy Spirit led me to Romans 14:13, *"Therefore let us not judge one another any more, but rather determine this—not to put an obstacle or stumbling block in a brother's way."*

This is the principle the Holy Spirit taught me from this verse. Repentance was not being sorry that I failed and hurt my wife and daughters. What I came to realize was that I had been an obstacle, an obstacle in my wife and daughter's lives. That truth motivated me to genuinely repent.

Step 4: Be aware of wrong wording. I need to stop here and give you five cautions for taking action.

> 1. Satan does not want you to do what is right. Many people are deceived into thinking if they are going to do what is right, there is nothing Satan can do. That is a lie straight from the pits of hell.
>
> 2. If you are going to do what is right, Satan will try to get you to use the wrong method.
>
> 3. If you are going to do what is right, using the right method, Satan will try to get you to do what is right in the wrong spirit or attitude. It is not what you say but how you say it.
>
> 4. If you are going to do what is right, using the right method, in the right spirit or attitude, Satan will try to get you to do it in the wrong timing.
>
> 5. If you are going to do what is right, using the right method, in the right spirit or attitude, and with the right timing, there is very little if anything that Satan can do about it. That is spirit-controlled living.

The biblical example of right wording is found in the parable of the prodigal son Luke 15:17-19, 21. Notice his words, *"But when he came to his senses, he said, 'How many of my father's hired men have more than enough bread, but I am dying here with hunger! I will get up and go to my father, and will say to him, "Father, I have sinned against heaven, and in your sight; I am no longer worthy to be called your son; make me as one of your hired men."' And the son said to him 'Father, I have sinned against heaven and in your sight; I am no longer worthy to be called your son."*

Nowhere does the prodigal son blame his father, mother or older brother. He didn't say "Dad, mom, if you had done so and so," or "if you hadn't done so and so, I wouldn't be in this mess. Just looks how you have ruined my life. It's all your fault!" He did not say to his older brother, "If you had not been so mean to me and laughed at me, I would not be in this pig pen. It is your fault I am in this terrible situation. You should have taken up and looked after me. It's all your fault!"

No! The prodigal son accepted complete responsibility for his actions and his predicament.

In restoring value to your spouse and children, your words must identify your specific offenses and reflect full repentance and humility. Correct wording will grow out of pure motives and attitudes. Correct wording draws attention to your offenses, not your spouses or children's offenses. Words that reflect blame will create additional problems in your relationships.

Remember the speck and beam principle? *"And why do you look at the speck in your brother's (spouse and/or children's) eye, but do not notice the log that is in your own eye? Or how can you say to your brother (spouse and/or children), 'Let me take the speck out of your eye,' and behold, the log is in your own eye? You hypocrite, first take the log out of you own eye; and then you will see clearly enough to take the speck out of your brother's (spouse and children's) eye."* Matthew 7:3-5

One principle that Jesus is teaching here is that what we see as major, others see as minor and what we see as minor, others see as major. In other words, our offenses will seem much greater to our spouse and children than they do us.

Examples of wrong wording:
- "I was wrong but you were too."
- "I'm sorry it happened, but it wasn't all my fault."
- "If I've been wrong, I hope you will forgive me."

These types of responses accept no responsibility for one's action. I am convinced that the three words Satan loves to hear Christians when they are confronted with a wrong are "I am sorry." What is one "sorry" for? Are they sorry for what they've done or that they've been caught? Most are sorry because they were caught. The three hardest words to say are "I was wrong."

I have also found it is much easier to say "Please forgive me," rather than ask "Will you forgive me?"

Step 5: Carefully select and use correct wording. An example of right wording: "God has convicted me of how wrong I was in (name your offense). Will you forgive me for the way I have treated you or for what I have done to you?"

In chapter 8, I told you the story of Eddie and Amanda and how after she got pregnant, he would not make love to his wife. Here's the rest of the story.

Eddie had quite a sexual history before meeting Amanda, however, Eddie was Amanda's first sexual experience. After explaining to Eddie how his sexual experiences was a sin against his soul and spirit and his marriage, I led him through the steps, which are described in Chapter 8. Once he experienced the healing of his soul and spirit, I taught him the principles of restoring value to Amanda. I emphasized that he must pray that the Holy Spirit would prepare Amanda to be receptive to his words and to following the principles for taking action.

Two weeks later, both Eddie and Amanda came to the session. The first words out of Amanda's mouth were, "I don't know what you've done to Eddie, but for the past week he hasn't been able to keep his hands off me."

"Are you bragging or complaining?" I asked. She replied with a smile, "I'm not complaining."

I asked her to share with me what had transpired since the last session I had with Eddie. Read carefully what she said. "Over the weekend, Eddie said he needed to talk to me. He told me that God had convicted him of how wrong he had been in having sex with other women and with me before marriage. He realized he had devalued me and had sinned not only against me, but also against God, the marriage and himself. He said, 'I don't deserve your forgiveness for my sexual sin, but will you forgive me for sinning against you and our marriage?'"

I asked Amanda what she felt when he ask for her forgiveness. "Blair, for the first time in our relationship I felt unconditional love and acceptance and I forgave Eddie."

I then asked Eddie what he felt. "Blair, when I accepted her forgiveness and thanked her for forgiving me, I can't describe what I felt inside of me. It was as if I became a new person. I had a desire to make love to my wife like no desire I've every known before."

The next words he spoke were words I had never heard before, or since. "Blair, when we made love it was spiritual experience. It was like we were really one for the first time."

When Eddie claimed healing for his soul and spirit due to his sexual sin and restored value to his wife, God preformed a miracle not only in their lives but in their marriage as well.

An important principle to grasp here is that the primary purpose in asking for forgiveness is not to restore a relationship but to make your way pleasing to God. It is possible that the person you are asking to forgive you cannot at that point. One of the reasons is that if they have wronged you in some way, they cannot forgive unless they are willing to take responsibility for their actions. Another reason may be that their hurt is so deep, that they are not sure of your sincerity and as a result, some time must elapse before they can forgive. Remember, forgiveness does not automatically restore a broken relationship.

Chapter 14 *Restoring One's Value*

When I made the decision to allow God to rebuild my life and marriage, I knew I had to ask several people to forgive me. That group of people not only included my wife but my two daughters, Shannon and Amy, as well. Guess whom the last ones were that I asked for forgiveness? You guess it, my two daughters.

On the Saturday morning before I started my profession as a counselor, I met with my daughters individually. I met with the oldest, Shannon, first. I told her how God had convicted me of how wrong I was to walk out on her, her mother and sister. I was wrong for not being at home for her first date. I was wrong for being self-centered and only looking out for my desires and ignoring by responsibilities as a father.

I then said, "I don't deserve your forgiveness, but will you forgive your dad for walking out on you, your mother and sister and not being here when you needed me?"

Shannon relied, "Yes, daddy I forgive you."

The Holy Spirit led me to take another step that I have not shared with you. I said to Shannon, "I don't ask that you love and respect me as your dad because I don't deserve it. But will you give me the opportunity to earn your love and respect?"

I will never forget that moment; Shannon put her arms around my neck and said, "Yes, daddy, I'll give you the opportunity to earn my love and respect."

I went through the same steps with my youngest daughter, Amy. The results were the same. You may be wondering if I was able to earn my daughters' love and respect again. The answer to that question is "yes."

When my son-in-law, Michael, asked Shannon to marry him, her response was, "Not until you ask my dad." That is what I call respect.

When Michael and Shannon had their first child, Tanner, I will never forget the emotions I felt when they asked me to do the dedication service for Tanner. I am convinced beyond any doubt that this would never have happened if I had not humbled myself before my daughters and restored value to them.

Did I earned Amy's love and respect? Yes! I could not ask for any greater love and respect than what Amy and Shannon have demonstrated over the past twelve years.

Please take note: the primary purpose in asking another for forgiveness is **NOT** to receive forgiveness, but to make your way pleasing to God. You may be led by the Holy Spirit to ask another to forgive you and they say "no" or "I can't at this time" or some other negative response. Your response here should be something like, "I hope and pray that in time you will be able to forgive me for my actions against you." Your freedom results from being obedient to God, not in how one respond to you.

Step 6. After having asked for forgiveness, it is important that you verbally accept the forgiveness from the one who is forgiving you and to thank them for forgiving you. The reason is that Satan and his demons cannot read your mind or know your thoughts. Only God is all knowing. By not verbally accepting the forgiveness, the one who forgives has no assurance that their forgiveness was accepted.

The steps mentioned in this chapter on restoring one's value are crucial if you hope to establish and maintain a fulfilling marriage and family relationship. The principle given to us in Matthew 5:23-24 *"If therefore you are presenting your offering (gift) at the altar, and there remember that your brother has something against, leave your offering (gift) there before the altar, and go your way, first be reconciled to your brother, and then come and present your offering (gift),"* is still relevant for today.

Chapter 15

Forgiveness: The Key to A Fulfilling Relationship

The key that finalized the healing in my life, marriage and ministry was that learning and applying the principles of forgiveness. I preached and taught the Bible for almost seventeen years and many of those sermons and lessons dealt with forgiveness. However, it was only as I worked through the emotional wounds in my life under the leadership of the Holy Spirit that I came to a clearer understanding of the dynamics of forgiveness.

From having worked with hundreds of couples over the past eleven years, I am convinced that an unforgiving spirit is a major cause of conflict in marriage and family relationships or in any relationship.

The principles I share with you in this chapter are the ones God taught and led me to apply in my own life and as well as principles he has taught me in working with individuals and couples.

Richard and Lisa, who had been married less than six months came in for counseling. This was his second marriage and her third. Their problem was his possessiveness and jealousy. Lisa's first two marriages ended due to spousal abuse. Richard's first marriage ended because of him catching his wife in his bed with another man. After revealing this information to me, he said "If you are going to tell me I have to forgive my ex-wife for what she did, you can forget it. I will never forgive her even if it means this marriage ends in divorce."

He then walked out of my office and I never saw them again. I am convinced the reason for his extreme jealously was due to his unforgiving spirit toward his ex-wife.

The Bible has a lot to say about forgiveness.

Matthew 18: 21-35, "Then Peter came to Him and said, 'Lord, how often

Chapter 15   *Forgiveness: The Key to A Fulfilling Relationship*

shall my brother sin against me, and I forgive him? Up to seven times?' Jesus said to him, 'I do not say to you, up to seven times, but up to seventy times seven. Therefore, the kingdom of heaven is like a certain king who wanted to settle accounts with his servants. And when he had begun to settle accounts one was brought to him who owed him ten thousand talents ($10,000,000). However, as he was not able to pay, his master commanded that he be sold, with his wife, children, and all he had, and that payment be made. The servant there fell down before him, saying, 'Master, have patience with me, and I will pay you all.' Then the master of that servant was moved with compassion - released him, and forgave him the debt. But that servant went out and found one of his fellow servants who owed him a hundred denari; ($20.00) and he laid hands on him and took him by the throat, saying, 'Pay me what you owe!' So his fellow servant fell down at his feet and begged him saying, 'Have patience with me, and I will pay you all. 'And he would not, but went and threw him into prison until he should pay the debt. Therefore, when his fellow servants saw what had been done, they were very grieved, and came and told their master all that had been done. Then his master, after he had called him, said to him, 'You wicked servant! I forgave you all that debt ($10,000,000) because you begged me. Should you not also have had compassion on your fellow servant, just as I had pity on you?' And his master was angry, and delivered him to the torturers until he should pay all that was due to him. So My heavenly Father also will do to you if each of you, from his heart, does not forgive his brother his trespasses."

Matthew 6:14 & 15, "For if you forgive men their trespasses, your Heavenly Father will also forgive you. But if you do not forgive men their trespasses, neither will your Father forgive your trespasses."

Luke 6:37, "Forgive, and you will be forgiven."

Luke 17:3 & 4 "Take heed to yourselves. If your brother sins against you, rebuke him; and if he repents, forgive him. And if he sins against you seven times in a day, and seven times in a day returns to you, saying, 'I repent,' you shall forgive him."

Ephesians 4:32 "And be kind to one another, tender-hearted, forgiving one another, just as God in Christ also forgave you."

John 20:22-23 "And when He had said this, He breathed on them, and said to them, 'Receive the Holy Spirit. If you forgive the sins of any, they are forgiven them; if you retain the sins of any, they are retained.'"

The Holy Spirit took me through four steps in the area of forgiveness and He has led me to use these same steps with those whom I counsel. Those steps are:

1. We must ask for and accept forgiveness from the Lord Jesus Christ.

2. We must ask those we sinned against to forgive us.

3. We must forgive those who sinned against us.

4. We must be willing to forgive ourselves.

Step one: We must ask for and accept forgiveness from the Lord Jesus Christ. If you have read this far and not accepted Christ as your personal Savior, I urge you to do so. Christ is the only answer for true peace and happiness in any relationship. How do you accept Christ as Lord and Savior in your life? Pray the following prayer from your heart: "Lord Jesus, I confess all my sins and I repent of all my sins. I do not want to do them anymore. I believe that you died on the cross in order that my sins can be forgiven. Will you forgive me of my sins? Based on your word in I John 1:9, you said, 'If I confess my sins that you will be faithful and just to forgive me of my sins', I accept your forgiveness of all my sins. Thank you for forgiving me of all my sins. Right now on this, the (day of the month, year and time), I receive you into my heart and life as Lord and Savior. Thank you Lord Jesus for coming into my life. Amen."

Step two: We must ask those we sinned against to forgive us. This step must be taken under the leadership of the Holy Spirit. Chapter 12 (previous chapter) gives the guidelines for this step.

Step three: We must forgive those who sinned against us.

One of the first principles God taught me about forgiveness is that it is rooted in the mercy, faithfulness and justice of God. Then He taught me that forgiveness was an act of the will, not based on my feeling. You will recall that the feeling of love return to me for my wife because of me acting on my will (see pages 27-30).

I was counseling with a man who was struggling in the area of forgiving some people who had inflicted deep hurt upon him. As I shared with him the principle of forgiving by will, he said, "I can't even will to forgive."

I asked him if he was willing to be made willing to forgive. He replied, "I can pray that prayer."

For several months he prayed, "Lord, I am willing to be made willing to forgive."

I will never forget the day he walked into my office and said, "Blair, I will to forgive those people for hurting me."

When I asked him what his next step of action would be, he responded, "On my way home, I'm going to stop and ask the leader of that group to forgive me for my wrong attitude toward them. Will you pray with me that God will not only give me the right words but also prepare his heart to be open to forgive me."

Before he left that day, I taught him how to apply the principle of restoring value. The next day he called and shared the peace that he experienced because of forgiving those who had hurt him.

You may be thinking at this point, "He or she does not deserve forgiveness. You just don't know what they did to me." That may be true from the human perspective. But listen, none of us deserve the Lord's forgiveness! That is the point I believe Christ was making in the parable found in Matthew 18: 21-35.

You may also be thinking, "if I forgive them, I'm letting them off the hook." Forgiving your offender is not letting them off the hook; it is letting yourself off the hook. I can tell you from personal experience, there is peace, joy, freedom and power in forgiving those who sinned against us. Remember this principle: **Forgiveness is a choice and the result is freedom!**

Again, John 20:23 said, "If you forgive the sins of any, they are forgiven them; if you retain the sins of any, they are retained." Allow me to paraphrase this verse. "When you forgive the sins of others, they are released. When you do not forgive the sins of others, they are retained." Until you choose to forgive those who sinned against you, they have power and control over you. Once you choose to forgive that power is broken. Not only is the power broken, but Satan also loses a weapon he can use for personal attacks.

As the Holy Spirit guided me through the steps of forgiveness, I began to discover that forgiveness opens my spirit, whereas unforgiveness causes me to have a closed spirit.

What is forgiveness? One thing I learned about forgiveness is that it is not excusing. Forgiveness is not saying, "Well, they couldn't help it, or they didn't really mean to do it." The Holy Spirit taught me that forgiveness is acknowledging that I had been hurt and been sinned against. However, as Christ chose to forgive me, I also choose to forgive those who sinned against me.

What happens when we forgive? Let me to share with you what happened in my life when I forgave. First, I let go of my resentment. The desire to punish them was no longer present. I placed them in the Lord's hand. Then I found myself being able pray for them. I was able to identify with their pain. As I forgave others, I began to see how emotional wounds inflict more wounds that are emotional. Again, I want to remind you that as you forgive by will, a release of feelings will come in time, and this amount of time varies from person to person.

You may be thinking at this point, "Okay, I'm supposed to forgive, and it's by my will not my feelings. So, how do I forgive?

First, we must ask for and accept God's unconditional forgiveness. If you have not done this, pray from your heart the prayer on page 50.

Second, ask the Holy Spirit and give Him permission to empower you to forgive by will.

Third, pray the following prayer from your heart: Dear Heavenly Father, thank You for Your love that was manifested in the sending of Your only Son, Jesus Christ, to die on the cross and while dying on the cross to pray, "Father forgive them for they know not what they do." I thank you for forgiving me of all my sins. I confess that I have not extended the same love and forgiveness toward others who have offended and hurt me, but instead I have harbored bitterness and anger. I ask and give you permission to reveal to me those individuals I need to forgive in order that I may make my way pleasing to You. I pray this prayer in the precious name of the Lord Jesus Christ, with thanksgiving. Amen."

Where does one start the process of forgiveness? For each person it is different. I had to start with my father. I then dealt with other significant individuals as the Holy Spirit led me.

One principle that I have learned over the years regarding forgiveness is that many individuals have forgiven from the head but not from the heart. What is the difference? To forgive from the head is saying, "Okay, I forgive." To forgive from the heart is to get into touch with the emotions we experienced because of the hurt. How does one go about getting in touch with the emotional pain especially when one is forgiving by will? The method I have felt led to use the most is one that I picked up from Paul Travis, who is associated with *Freedom in Christ* ministries. I have individuals make a list of people who have emotionally and spiritually hurt them. Beside their name, they identify specifically how they were hurt or wounded and how they felt. I then have them pray the following prayer: "Lord Jesus, as you have chosen to forgive me of all my sins, I choose by will to forgive (name the person) for (verbally state every hurt and pain and how it made you feel). I realize now that my attitude has affected my relationship with the Lord and is hindering my spiritual growth. Lord, I forgive (name) for (state the hurt and pain and how it made you feel). (Name) is now free, forgiven and is released. The debt (name) owes me is now cancelled and (name) owes me nothing further. Lord, I am going to fully trust you concerning the future. Satan, I take authority over you in the name of Jesus Christ and by the power of His resurrected life, I take back the ground I have allowed you to gain in my life because of my attitude toward (name) and give this ground back to my Lord Jesus Christ."

When the individual has forgiven every one on their list, I have them to complete this step by praying: "Lord, on this (day, date and time), I release all these people and myself to You and my right to seek revenge. I choose not to hold on to my bitterness and anger and I ask You to heal my damaged emotions. I not only ask for this healing but I accept Your healing of my damaged emotions on this (day, date and time). I pray this prayer in Jesus' name with thanksgiving. Amen"

In come cases I have had individuals to write a love letter to the one who hurt and wounded them. The format I use is one I that was presented at a sexual abuse seminar I attended several years ago. The format was reprinted in part from *What You Heal, You Can Feel*, by John Gray, Ph.D. To write a love letter begin by expressing your angry feelings, your long-held resentments, and your blame. I tell the individual to address their letter just like any other letter they are writing. For many as they moved through each step, they found freedom and healing.

STEP 1: Anger and Blame

>I did not like it when. . .
>
>I resent . . .
>
>I hate it when you . . .
>
>I want . . .

STEP 2: Hurt and Sadness

>I feel sad when you . . .
>
>I hurt because . . .
>
>I want . . .

STEP 3: Fear and Insecurity

    I feel afraid when . . .
    I am scared you will . . .
    I feel scared because . . .
    I want . . .

STEP 4: Guilt and Responsibility

    I am wrong for . . .
    I wish . . .
    I did not mean to . . .

STEP 5: Love, Forgiveness and Thankfulness

    I love you because . . .
    I forgive you for . . .
    I thank you for . . .

The purpose of the love letter is to allow the real feelings to surface so there can be healing. Some individuals shared their letter with the person they were writing to. If this is not an option, I have them share it with a trusted friend or me. It was only as I got in touch with the emotional pain of my wounds that I was able to establish and maintain a forgiving spirit.

A fourth step I have used with some individuals is to have them meditate and talk about the words Christ spoke on the cross "Father forgive them for they know not what they do." This is the step the Holy Spirit led me to take in being able to forgive the man who sexually molested me as a child.

Why did Jesus pray on the cross "Father forgive the for they know not what they do?" To answer that question we need to go to Matthew's gospel, chapter 24, verses 24 and 25: *"And when Pilate saw that he was accomplishing nothing, but rather that a riot was starting, he took water and washed his hands in front of the multitude, saying, 'I an innocent of this Man's blood; see to that yourselves. And all the people answered and said, 'His blood be on us and on our children.'"*

I am convinced that if the Jews had known all the future consequences of their actions, they would have never crucified Christ. In 70 AD, Titus, a Roman general, entered Jerusalem; 600,000 Jews were killed, and thousands were led into captivity. In 134 AD, Bar Cochba lead a rebellion against Roman rule. It was crushed. Jerusalem was leveled and the foundations of the walls were plowed up. During Hitler's rule in Germany, six million Jews were killed during the Holocaust. Had the Jews known all this was going to happen, do you feel they would have had Jesus crucified? No!

What was the reason for the Jews action? They wanted a Messiah to deliver them from Roman oppression without themselves having to change, and when Jesus did not fulfill their wishes, they became so angry and disgusted they did not even consider the consequences of their actions.

That is when the Holy Spirit revealed to me that if my molester had known the consequences of his actions on my life, he would have never molested me. The Holy Spirit enabled me to reflect on the emotional pain that my molester must have been experiencing in his own life to do such a terrible deed to me. I began to weep, not just for me but for him also. It was then that I was able to forgive him for molesting me.

A lesson that I feel we must learn is that the majority of those who offend us or sin against us does so not because they wake up one day and decided to sin against us. Their sin is a result of the sins against them in their own lives. Does this give them an excuse? **Absolutely not!** They are still responsible for their actions just as we are responsible to forgive them for their actions. We are also responsible for our own sins, and we are blessed that we always know that Jesus will forgive us if we ask.

Fifth, in order to forgive you may have to confront the one who wronged and sinned against you. I was counseling a woman, Janice, who had been raped by an uncle when she was thirteen. She never revealed his name. She was struggling with whether or not she had really forgiven him. As we discussed the various aspects of forgiveness, I asked her, "If you have forgiven someone, should you be able to tell them that you have forgiven them for their actions against you?"

Her response was, "I know what you are saying, but I'm not sure I can confront my uncle."

I asked her if she would be willing to express forgiveness to her uncle if the Holy Spirit empowered her and provided the right opportunity. She said, "I'm willing, however, the Lord would have to really give me the strength to confront my uncle."

When Janice came in for her next session, she began to weep. I asked her about the tears. When she had regained her composure, she told me the following story. "This past weekend, the family had gathered at my parents home. For the first time I became aware that my uncle always isolated himself from the rest of the family. Most of the family was in the family room, but my uncle was in the kitchen, alone. Blair, the Holy Spirit moved me out of my chair into the kitchen and I told my uncle that I forgave him for raping me."

I asked, "What was his response?"

Janice said, "He broke down and cried and said, 'do you really forgive me?' and I said yes. He went on to say that there had been several times when he had wanted to confess and ask for forgiveness but was afraid he would have to go to jail. He asked again, do you really forgive me and again I assured him of my forgiveness. Blair you will never know what peace came over me in those moments."

By being willing to confront her uncle, Janice not only was freed from being raped, but she also enabled her uncle to experience forgiveness and freedom.

Please allow me to make this point very clear. I am NOT saying you have go confront the ones who sinned against you. What I am saying is that we need to be willing to confront them if God leads in that direction. The reason I emphasize this point is that I have never been led to confront and forgive my molester. The reason, I am not sure. The only reason that comes to my mind is that I know the man and with one phone call I could find where he lives. I do know that today he is a leader in his community and church. It is very possible that he blocked that experience out of his conscious. I have told the Lord if he ever wanted me to confront him, I was willing. To date that has not happened.

There is another important principle that must be learned. What do you feel I have been doing in my spirit while I have been writing about my molestation? Feeling bitter, angry, resentful and wanting revenge? No! I have been forgiving my molester all over again in my spirit. Maintaining this forgiving spirit keeps the bitterness, resentment, anger and seeking revenge from creeping back into my life. Can we love, forgive and pray for those who sin against us? Not in our humanness, but we can through Christ's redemptive love. God gives us freedom in our relationships through forgiveness. Forgiveness brings compassion and that is a miracle!

Ed Cole, shared in a message he delivered, "Forgiveness is the evidence of true holiness. God is holy. Holiness is manifested in love, which is an act of the will. Love is manifested by grace. The essence of grace is to show mercy.

Mercy is revealed in forgiveness."

Remember this principle: Forgiveness is not forgetting. Each time we remember, we need to forgive all over again. When we forgive, we do so never to use it against them again. Forgiveness allows us to embrace our past and be free of our past whether the past be moments or years ago.

Notice the freedom that results from forgiveness. Our hearts are set free from bitterness, resentment, anger and hatred. When we choose to forgive, we are able to become a channel of God's love and forgiveness to people who are starved for love and unconditional acceptance. The man mentioned in Matthew 18:21-35 missed this opportunity. Let us review the story. This man owed his master a huge debt and was unable to pay when the note came due. He pleaded for more time and the master had compassion and forgave him his debt. He then in turn went out and found a man who owed him a small debt and demanded payment. This man also begged for mercy and time but his request was denied. What would be the reason a man who had been forgiven a huge debt would refuse to forgive a small debt?

Matthew 18:26 reads, "Have patience with me and I will pay you all." Notice the response in verse 27. "And the lord of that slave felt compassion and released him and forgave him the debt."

What was the first thing this man did after he was forgiven? Did he rejoice? There is no record of him rejoicing. He went out to collect his accounts receivable. Think about this for a moment. If the institution holding the mortgage on your home called in the total payment and you were unable to pay the mortgage in full, would you plead for more time? Sure, we all would. Suppose that lender had mercy and forgave you the debt and marked on your deed, paid in full, what would be one of the first things you would do? In all probability, you would call your spouse, sharing the great news.

I am convinced based on this man's action, that when he heard "forgiven" he understood it as what he asked for which was more time. He failed to comprehend his unconditional forgiveness because he did not ask for forgiveness.

An additional lesson in this story is that many times we miss the blessings of God because we are focusing on what we asked Him. When we do not get what we ask for, many times we miss what God has given us instead. So many times, what God gives us is far greater than what we ask.

Notice the results of his unforgiveness (verse 34)
- His forgiveness was revoked.
- He was separated from his fellow servants.

- He was separated from his family.
- He was separated from his Master.

What happens when we fail to forgive?

- Your forgiveness stops. Look at Matthew 18:35 *"So shall My Heavenly Father also do to you, if each of you does not forgive his brother* (spouse) *from your heart."* Matthew 6:15 says *"If you do not forgive men their trespasses, neither will your Father forgive your trespasses."* What I see we are being taught here is that we come under bondage to what we do not forgive. In other words, God will not forgive in us what we refuse to forgive in the lives of others.
- You are separated from your friends.
- It will separate you and put up walls in your family relationships.
- You miss the full blessings of God by being out of fellowship with Him.

Here is the principle: Forgiveness is unconditional!

When we choose to forgive, we are able to demonstrate Christ-like qualities in our life. One Christ-like quality is found in Luke 17:4 *"And if he sins against you seven times a day, and returns to you seven times saying, 'I repent,' forgive him."* This is not easily accomplished.

True, forgiveness gives freedom. However, the forgiveness process is not always painless. Forgiveness in many situations opens infected wounds. Only clean wounds can be properly healed. The first step to healing is cleansing, however painful that me be.

Several years ago, in a softball game, I slid into a base, severely skinning up my leg. As the wound starting healing, I noticed the color surrounding the wound started changing. It kept getting worse. Rather than going to the doctor and inconveniencing him with such a trifling matter, I went instead to a pharmacist. I told him I thought my leg was infected and upon seeing it, he agreed. I asked him what I needed to do to solve my problem. He responded by saying I needed to remove the scab and clean the wound so it would heal properly. I proceeded to ask him how I would do that. He told me to put peroxide on the scab so that it would dissolve. Being brave, I asked him if it would hurt. He said, "No." He gave me an antiseptic to spray on the wound once the scab was removed. The next question I asked was "Will it burn?" He replied, "Oh no. It might sting a little." I went home and followed his directions. I was very cautious in applying the peroxide because I did not quite trust his opinion. True to his word, the peroxide did not hurt or burn at all. It was amazing to watch as the peroxide cleansed the infection from the wound. I thought, this is a piece of cake. Without testing the antiseptic to see if it would burn or not, I just sprayed the entire wound. If what I experienced was stinging, I do not ever want to know what burning would be like. It burned so badly, that I yelled and cried, scaring my family. However, after a few moments, the pain started subsiding and was completely gone. The wound then healed in a proper fashion.

Similarly, the healing process of our life can be painful. However, the pain is short-lived and healing will result. Here is a principle we need to remember about healing. Severe wounds leave scars. Some may fade while others remain visible. Scars are a reminder of healing, not that the wound still exists. In other words, forgiveness is a choice, forgetting is a process.

Remember, forgiveness in not forgetting, forgetting is a process.

The fourth step in forgiveness is that we must be willing to forgive ourselves. A common thing with many of us is to ask God to forgive us of our sins, yet we do not forgive ourselves. By not forgiving ourselves, we are holding that sin or sins against us. As a result we carry grudges against ourselves. When we refuse to forgive ourselves, we are placing ourselves under bondage of our sins and failures.

When we have asked God to forgive us, and He does when we ask, and we do not forgive ourselves, we have made ourselves greater than God. No one has the right not to forgive themselves when God has forgiven them. Forgiving yourself is accepting God's cleansing and healing.

My first day in the counseling center is a day I will never forget. As I was preparing for my first clients, Satan jumped on my shoulder and in my mind said, "Blair, who do you think you are being a marriage counselor? When people hear how you walked out on your wife and two daughters, not just once, but twice, you will not have any credibility. In fact, you being here will destroy the credibility of this counseling center. Just think of what people will say about you when they hear you walked out on your family just after your daughter finished her chemotherapy for cancer. You will be the laughing stock of the community."

I found myself buying into the lies of Satan and was ready to walk out of the center and never counsel with anyone. Then the Holy Spirit spoke to me in my mind and said, "Didn't the Lord Jesus forgive you?"

I replied, "Yes."

He then said, "Didn't your wife and daughters forgive you?"

Again, I replied, "Yes."

The question then changed. "Why haven't you forgiven yourself?"

In an audible voice I said, "Blair, I choose by will to forgive you for walking out on your wife and daughters and not being there for them when you were needed as a husband and father. The Lord Jesus loved you enough to forgive you, your wife and daughters loved you enough to forgive you and I love you enough to forgive you. On this Monday, May 16, 1988 I not only forgive you but I accept your forgiveness."

I did not feel a thing when I finished forgiving myself. A short time later that day, Satan jumped on my shoulder and started the same old attack. Immediately I responded back, "Satan, in the name of the Lord Jesus Christ, I rebuke you and command you out of this place. You have no authority over me for I am a child of God who has all authority in the name of Jesus. However, before you leave, I just want to thank you for reminding me of what I have been forgiven. Not only have I been forgiven by the Lord Jesus, my wife and daughters but at 10:35 a.m. on this Monday morning, May 16, 1988, I forgive and accepted my forgiveness." By no means am I a singer. However, I sang the chorus "Praise your name Lord Jesus, praise your name Lord Jesus. You are my rock, You are my fortress, You are my deliverer, and in You will I trust. Praise Your name Lord Jesus." Words cannot describe the feelings I experienced at that moment. Again, I remind you of the principle, as you act on your will, God will release the feelings in His time according to your needs.

In June of 1982, my daughter Amy, age 9, was diagnosed with Ewing's Sarcoma. She finished her cancer treatments in January of 1984. For the next 16 years, she was cancer free. On July 3, 2000, the cancer resurfaced. On March 7, 2001, Amy entered NC Baptist Hospital for the last time. During the last hours of her life, Amy wanted to be held. Each family member took turns holding her. As I held my daughter in my arms, I silently asked the Holy Spirit to reveal to me if there were any unresolved issues between my daughter and me. An overwhelming peace came over me as the Holy Spirit revealed that all issues had been resolved between Amy and me.

Why did I share that? You may be reading this book and realize there are unresolved issues between you and a family member. You know you need to ask for forgiveness or need to forgive, but for some reason have failed to do so. Life is uncertain. I urge you to take responsibility for the unresolved issues that my be present between you and a family member so that you can have a fulfilling marriage and family relationship and avoid facing the loss of a family member with unresolved issues.

Establishing and maintaining a forgiving spirit is the key to fulfilling marriage and family relationship.

PART FIVE:

BUILDING A FAMILY TEAM

Chapter 16

Recognize, Understand And Value Each Family Member

Then the Lord God said, "It is not good for the man to be alone; I will make him a helper suitable for him." **Genesis 3:18**

As I reflect back on the first seventeen years of my marriage, I can see that one of the major problems I had was I was constantly trying to change my wife. I wanted her to think the way I thought, to see my perceptions as I saw them, to act, perform and behave in the in the manner I chose for her. My problem was that I had developed a self-centered vision of what the marriage should be. As a result, we had major conflict, because Glenda also had a distorted vision of the marriage relationship.

Conflict is a fact of life. It has been present since the fall of man in the Garden of Eden and will remain with us until we get to heaven. The question is, do we allow conflict to rise above us or do we rise above conflict? As the eagle rises above the turbulence in the air, we can rise above the marital conflict we face day to day. To rise above conflict, first of all we need to apply the biblical principles, under the leadership of the Holy Spirit, that have been presented thus far and the ones being shared in the remainder of the book.

Every one of us is a unique creation. We are all unique individuals. When we get married or rather when we got married, we began to discover all the unique qualities about our spouse. Because of these unique, different qualities, we find ourselves trying to change our spouse so they will think the way we want them to think, see our perceptions as we want them to see our perceptions and behave, act or perform the way we want them to behave, act or perform. If we aren't careful, this will result in conflict that, if not managed or controlled, will eventually destroy the marriage and family relationship.

The Bible has several things to say about spouses living together in harmony with one another:

Chapter 16 Recognize, Understand And Value Each Family Member

Colossians 3:15 "Let the peace of Christ rule in your heart to which indeed you were called in one body." (NSAB)

II Corinthians 13:11 "Be of the same agreeable mind with one another." (AMP)

Romans 14:9 "So let us then definitely aim for and eagerly pursue what makes for harmony and for mutual up-building, edification, and development of one another." (AMP)

I Peter 3:7 "Husbands, in the same way be considerate as you live with your wives, and treat them with respect." (NIV) One translation says, "Live with your wives with understanding." We can paraphrase this to read, "Live with your wife and children with understanding."

Many spouses say, "I don't understand my wife or husband or my children." Part of our calling is to understand our spouse, children and ourselves.

Conflict exists because something is missing; like a piece of a puzzle.

Entire books have been written on the subject of dealing with and handling conflict. In this section, I am devoting four chapters, dealing with what I have found to be basic principles in rising above conflict.

Should I try to list all the reasons conflict exist, that too, would be an entire book. Some major causes of conflict that I have seen not only in my life, but also in the lives of many couples I have worked with, are as follows:

- Rejecting what one does not understand or comprehend, even if it is the truth.
- When one spouse expects the other spouse to recognize, what their needs are and refuse to communicate their needs.
- When parents expect their children to know to do certain things without clear communication.
- When a spouse tries to change their spouse by offering unsolicited advice.
- When a spouse/parents acknowledge what has not been done, rather than focus on what has been done.
- When a husband and wife do not recognize, understand and value their personality differences.
- When a husband and/or wife gain an understanding of their differences, but refuse to accept the differences.

Proverbs 19:13 "...a quarrelsome wife (husband) is like a constant dripping."

Proverbs 21:9 "Better to live on a corner of the roof that share a house with a quarrelsome wife (husband)."

Proverbs 30: 21 & 23 "Under three things the earth trembles, under four it cannot bear up.... An unloved woman (man) who is married..."

Why do we endure conflict? We endure conflict so we can win, be stronger, and bring positive results. When a marriage and family learns to deal with conflict, the family bonds. The attitude will be, "we'll get through this and be better off." A family with no conflict is not bonded.

At one time or another you have heard the statement, "opposites attract." Dr. Robert Rohm adds, "then they attack." Why is this? Two people are making the same decision. One makes his decision based on facts and principles, while the other makes the same decision according to feelings and self-expression. What are they going to find? Conflict.

Since conflict is a fact of life and a regular part of our relationship, how do we handle it? What steps can we take to rise above conflict, rather than conflict rising above us? Isaiah 40:31, "Yet those who wait for the Lord will gain new strength; they will mount up with wings like eagles, they will run and not get tired, they will walk and not become weary." Blair's paraphrase, "Yet those who learn to handle conflict will gain new strength; they will mount up with wings like eagles, they will run and not get tired, they will walk and not become weary."

The most important truth I have learned in the area of handling conflict in the family is the importance of not only understanding me, but also understanding my wife and children.

When a relationship starts out, each person values attributes or characteristics that are attractive in the other person as well as some differences. Because the attractive traits out-weigh these small differences, we are willing to tolerate these small differences. As we tolerate these differences, we believe that in time the other person will get smarter or learn from our example or just figure things out for themselves. People do this without understanding their personality style blend.

In graduate school, I was exposed to several personality profiles, which had little if any impact on my life. However, when I was exposed to the **DISC** personality profile, my life, marriage and ministry have not been the same. Outside of my salvation and the principles God has taught me from the Bible, what I've learned about my own personality and my families' personality through the **DISC** model taught to me by Dr. Robert Rohm of Personality Insights is the greatest knowledge I possess. It has been a valuable tool in handling conflict within my family unit as well as in other

Chapter 16 *Recognize, Understand And Value Each Family Member*

relationships.

What I learned was I have predictable patterns of behavior and they blend to give me, and each member of my family, a unique personality. That is also true for you, your spouse and children.

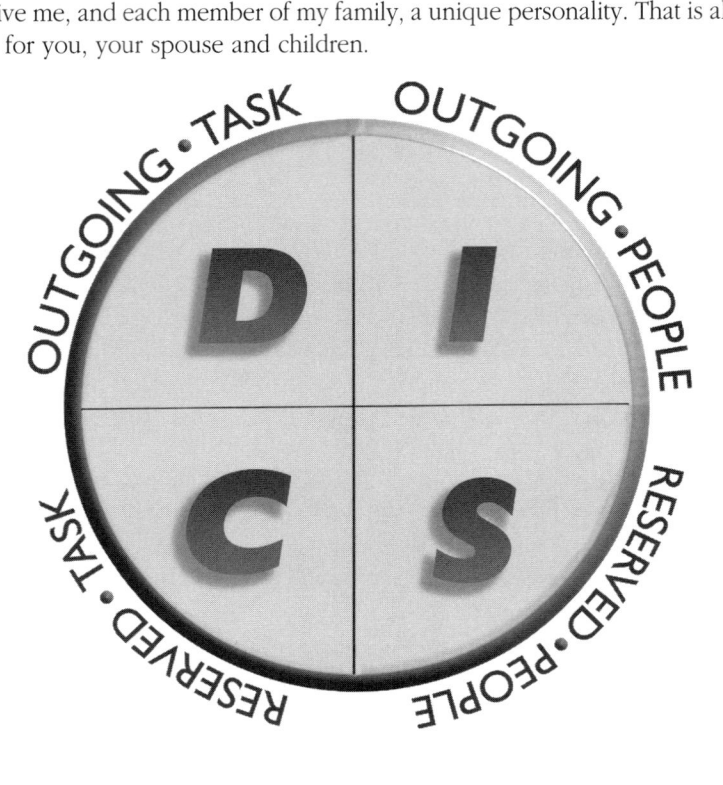

The personality types are like a circle. The top half of the circle represents **active/outgoing** type personality while the lower half of the circle represents the **passive/reserve** type. The left half of the circle represents the **task-oriented** individual and the right half of the circle the **people oriented** individual. The diagram illustrates the four parts, which represents four personality types. As you look at the diagram, you will notice each part of the circle has been labeled with a letter. The top left-hand quadrant is labeled "***D***", the top right hand quadrant is labeled "***I***", the lower right hand quadrant is labeled "***S***" and the lower left-hand quadrant is labeled "***C***". This picture of the circle has made it easy for me to remember what each part represents. The beauty of this model is that each major characteristic of each type starts with the letter located in that quadrant.

The "**D**" type individual tends to be *outgoing* and *task oriented - the upper left quadrant* of the circle. They tend to be dominant, **decisive, direct, demanding, determined, dogmatic, doers** and can be **defiant**. They may push the boundaries further than normal. They are very fast-paced and love challenging tasks. Their motto is "where there is a will, there is a way!"

The **D** type prefers to be in control of his environment. When making a decision, these individuals enjoy deciding not only for themselves...but for everyone else, too!

D type people also like to be in charge. They dislike the confinement of limited choices. They tend to speak bluntly, because they want to get to the bottom line quickly. They like competition and seek individual accomplishment.

The **I** type person also tend to be *outgoing* but they are noticeably more *people oriented*--the *upper right quadrant* of the circle. They are a lot of fun. They love to talk and joke. Generally, they are **inspiring, influencing, impressive, interesting, impressionable, important, interchangeable, interested in people** and can be **illogical**. These individuals are relational and can be very charismatic. Many of their decisions are based on emotions, which can cause them to make impulsive decisions, thus creating problems. Their motto is "it's party time, let the good times roll."

The **S** type person is *people oriented*, too, but they are more *reserved* - the *lower right quadrant* of the circle. This style is foreign to a **D** or I. However, research shows this style makes up 30-35% of the general population.

How can we recognize **S** type people in daily life? They are s**upportive, steady, stable, sweet, shy, status quo, sentimental, submissive** and at times a **sucker**. They do not like confrontation, but prefer peace at almost any cost. Perhaps that is why they can be a sucker. The hardest word for them to say is "No!"

They have an adaptable skill that seeks to provide whatever seems necessary (more or less) in order to create harmony and completion. Their driving passion is to feel appreciation, *security* and *approval*. They prefer stability and do not like change. They want everyone to be cooperative and get along with one another.

The **C** type person is also *reserved*, but they are *task oriented - bottom left quadrant* of the circle. Their traits are **cautious, correct, competent, critical thinking, careful, conscientious, calculating** and their weakness is that they can appear on the surface to be **cold**. You wonder if they have a "heart". However, after getting to know them you realize they do have a "warm" side to them.

Chapter 16   *Recognize, Understand And Value Each Family Member*

The **C** tends to know and follow the rules, and they expect everyone else to do the same! To them, conscientious attention and consistency are very important in every part of their life. Their "passion" is for *quality information, excellence* and good *value*. They are comfortable with details and charts. The **C** is a long-term thinker and can focus effectively on the smallest details. They are orderly people when taking on a task; finish it with preciseness thus earning respect. The C invented coloring inside the lines, whereas the **D** invented coloring outside the lines.

Of course, no one is purely just a "**D**", "**I**", "**S**", or "**C**" - each of us has a personal, measurable blend of all four traits, to a greater of lesser degree.

When my wife and I took the personality style analysis, we discovered that she was a primary "**S-C**" and secondary "**I**", making my wife an "**S-C-I**" blend. My profile revealed that my primary style was that of an "**I**" and my secondary style was a "**D**". My profile also revealed that my "**C**" was above the midline, making me a "**I-D-C**" blend.

The style of my wife revealed that she is steady, stable, supportive, sensitive, cautious, competent, careful, calculating and compliant. Her secondary style "kicks in" when she gets under pressure and she becomes inspiring, influencing, impressive and interested in people.

My personality style reveals that I am inspiring, influencing, interactive, impressive, interest in people, and at times illogical. My secondary style, which is a "**D**" reveals that under pressure I can be dominate, direct, demanding, decisive, determined and at times defiant.

DISC not only revealed the characteristics our personalities but also our strengths and weaknesses. We learned how we respond when under control and how we act when out of control. A major revelation for us was when we discovered that our weaknesses are actually strengths pushed to an extreme. For example:

My Strengths	**My Weaknesses**
Friendly	Weak-willed
Compassionate	Unstable
Carefree	Undisciplined
Talkative	Restless
Enthusiastic	Undependable
Practical	Inconsiderate
Strong-willed	Angry

Optimistic............................... Domineering

Her Strengths   **Her weaknesses**
Dependable............................... Fearful
Easygoing............................... Indecisive
Trustworthy............................... Spectator
Efficient............................... Self-Protective
Diplomatic............................... Timid
Humorous............................... Shy
Analytical............................... Moody
Perfectionist............................... Negative
Loyal............................... Impractical
Aesthetic............................... Rigid

The value of this information is to understand the reasons for our weaknesses and the steps we can take to improve those areas.

There have been many times in my life where I felt completely out of control and did not understand the reason why I demonstrating certain behaviors. The same is true of my wife. **DISC** has solved that problem for us. The chart below reveals our "under control" and "out of control" characteristics.

Under Control I Am   **Out of Control I Can Be**
Courageous............................... Reckless
Quick to respond............................... Rude
Goal-oriented............................... Impatient
Self-Confident............................... Conceited
Direct............................... Abrasive
Self-Reliant............................... Arrogant
Optimistic............................... Unrealistic
Persuasive............................... Manipulative
Excited............................... Emotional
Spontaneous............................... Impulsive
Outgoing............................... Unfocused
Involved............................... Directionless

Chapter 16   *Recognize, Understand And Value Each Family Member*

Under Control She Is	Out of Control She Can Be
Relaxed	Lacking Initiative
Reliable	Dependent
Stable	Indecisive
Softhearted	Easily Manipulated
Steadfast	Resistant to Change
Systematic	Slow
Single-Minded	Inflexible
Orderly	Compulsive
Logical	Critical
Curious	"Nosey"
Teachable	Easily Offended
Cautious	Fearful
Questioning	Doubtful
Conscientious	Worrisome
Precise	"Picky"

These strengths and weakness helped me to understand why at times I would be "higher than a kite" or "lower than a skunk." One major weakness I have known about all my life is in the area of self-discipline. I made the mistake that the majority of high "*I*'s" make by believing that talking and doing are synonymous. Understanding my **DISC** profile has enabled me to become more self-disciplined in my life. On the other hand I came to understand why helping others motivated my wife, yet at times it seems to both of us that she was simply being manipulated. I now understand why my wife is seldom in a hurry, stays with proven methods so things will be done correctly.

Understanding our personality styles has helped us to understand each other's basic needs. My wife's basic need in her personality style is appreciation, security and quality answers. My basic need is that of recognition, approval and control.

In the area of communication, **DISC** has taught me to communicate with my wife using the words "how" and "why". As an "*S*" she needs to know "how" it should be done or how we are we going do it. As a "*C*" she needs

144

to have quality answers. On the other hand, Glenda communicates with me using the words "who" and "what". I need to know "who" is involved, "who" is doing it and "what" the results will be.

DISC has also taught us what not to do in communicating. I learned that I could not do the following:

- Rush her in the decision-making process.
- Be domineering or demanding.
- Force her to respond quickly to what I want.
- Avoid using visual words.
- Make dogmatic statements
- Be overly excited about the issue or matter at hand.
- My wife has learned not to do the following when communicating with me:
- Talk down to me.
- Use too many audio words.
- Be dictatorial.

Notice how personality styles clash. The "**D**" wants to get the job done now; the "**I**" wants to have some fun and not be so serious about the task; the "**S**" wants to help, but in a slower pace; while the "**C**" wants the task done perfectly.

Two high "**D**'s" have conflict over who is in control; two high "**I**'s" have conflict with who gets the spotlight and all the attention. Two high "**S**'s" get along great but struggle if neither takes the initiative. Two high "**C**'s" have conflict over who is right.

In the area of conflict, it is easy to believe that the other person is trying to do something to us. The principle to remember is that most people are not trying to do something against us rather they are trying to do something for themselves.

The "**D**" spouse wants the job done now. The high "**I**" spouse wants to have some fun first.

When conflict arises with your spouse or children, think about what is causing the negative behavior or reaction. Do they remind you of a demanding parent when you were a child? Is your spouse or child like the sibling with whom you fought with a lot growing up? By understanding what pushes your hot button, you will be able to be more sensitive and

145

understanding in dealing with your own spouse and children. We need to learn how to respond, not react.

In addition, in handling disagreements, we need to understand how different personalities respond to conflict. The "*D*" demands that others do as they want and pushes them a little bit faster. If that does not work, they become overly assertive, autocratic and controlling, demanding his/her own way through forceful power. "They will demonstrate an attitude of, "Do it my way!" In the extreme, they work alone and move into an area that others cannot control. The "*I*'s" say "lighten up, have a good time." If that does not work, he will try even harder to talk you into doing it his/her way. If that does not work, they attack verbally and emotionally, trying to discredit others and their ideas. The "*S*" says, "relax a little, sit back. We'll get there." If that does not work, they tolerate and give up. In the extreme they think, "these guys can do all this running around, but I'm going to stay where I am and not move. We'll still be where I am when it's all over." In extreme situations, they may emotionally attack.

The "*C*" says, "pay closer attention to these details and get this right." He avoids conflict by withdrawing, ignoring or planning a new strategy and says, "I'll do it myself." He avoids confrontation when possible. If that does not work, they impose their high standard of "right" and "wrong" on everyone to demonstrate through facts and upholding principles that their way is right.

By understanding this, we are better able to respond positively and thoughtfully, rather than react negatively. Thus, we are able to make wiser decisions.

In dealing with conflict, realize that other family members do not think or act like you. "*D*'s" do not like to be told how to do things. They want the challenge and control to figure out how to do it for themselves. "*I*'s" need the freedom and flexibility to complete the task and have fun doing it. "*S*'s" need to be told how it needs to be done without being rushed. "*C*'s" need to know "why" and time to triple check their work.

Another principle in dealing with conflict is to make adjustments to meet your spouse and children's needs. "*D*'s" and "*I*'s" are fast paced; "*S*'s" and "*C*'s" are slower paced. Loving your spouse and children are not enough. Your love must soak in. They must feel loved. That means adjusting, adapting and accepting them, thus being better able to meet their needs. When you don't adjust and adapt your personality style blend, you can send the message that your spouse and/or children are a bother to you; that something is wrong with them because they are not like you. I have counseled many people whose parents loved them, but they never deeply experienced their parent's love.

No matter how different your spouse is, no matter how different and difficult your child seems to be, you must learn to adjust and adapt and accept them as the unique individuals they are.

It costs you energy to adjust and adapt to meet the needs of your family. As spouses and parents, we are asked to adjust and adapt in the way we relate to meeting the needs of each other as well as the needs of our children.

When we do this, we are pushed out of our comfort zone into thinking, perceiving and acting in a way that is not part of our natural personality style. The result is stress. Stress has a way of depleting our mental, emotional and physical energy. Low energy levels create impatience, lack of flexibility and behavior that is more obstinate. The lower one's energy level, the greater chances are for conflict with family members. By giving family members the opportunity to recharge their emotional batteries, the better the chance of reduced conflict.

"*D*'s" and "*C*'s" energy levels are drained when they have to move into a more people oriented interaction. "*I*'s" and "*S*'s" energy levels are drained when they are forced into a more task-oriented mode. "*S*'s" and "*C*'s" energy levels are drained when they are forced into a faster pace, while "*D*'s" and "*I*'s" are drained when they have to slow down. All this results in stress, which may be revealed in the following ways:

- "*D*'s" and "*I*'s" may become loud, demanding and hyperactive.
- "*S*'s" will usually get quiet and withdraw emotionally.
- "*C*'s" typically will start getting meticulous and whiney. They focus on something that bothers them and will not let go of it. Its almost like they get into a cycle and can't stop.

How do we recharge our emotional batteries?

1. Proper physical rest.
2. Recognize the various activities that help relieve stress and renew one's energy.
- "*D*'s" relieve stress by doing something physical; playing sports, working in the yard, etc.
- "*I*'s" recharge by being with people and talking to others.
- "*S*'s" recharge by doing something that requires very little energy; fishing, watching TV, sleeping, or taking a walk.
- "*C*'s" recharge by reading a book, listening to soft music or working

Chapter 16 *Recognize, Understand And Value Each Family Member*

on a project. They need time to be alone so they can think and process things.

Children have a harder time coping with their circumstances that are contrary to their personality style blend. They tend to be more self-centered and harder to get along with. When their energy level is high, they are able to cope better in uncomfortable situations. After a day at school, "***S***" and "***C***" children may be worn out from having to interact with others all day and need time to be alone and recharge. "***D***" and "***I***" children arrive home ready for action. They have been sitting all day in a structured, routine atmosphere and have energy to burn. It can be a mistake to force "***D***" and "***I***" children to do homework before they can go out and play or before the "***I***" has a chance to talk to someone. "***I***'s" get their energy level from other people.

By discovering what recharges your spouse and children's energy levels, you are then better able to adjust and adapt in meeting their needs.

As individuals, we also need to place a high priority on giving ourselves a regular time to recharge our mental, emotional and physical batteries as well as our own spiritual batteries. A key principle to remember - we cannot nurture others in the way we nurture ourselves.

Proverbs 22:6, calls on parents to nurture their children according to the child's personality style blend.

Chuck Swindoll said, "If parents were to ask me, 'What is the greatest gift we could give our child' . . . my counsel to you would be, give your child the time it takes to find out how he or she is put together. Help your child know who he or she is. Discuss those things with your children. Help them to know themselves so that they learn to love and accept themselves as they are. Then, as they move into a society that seems so committed to pounding them into another shape, they will remain true to themselves, secure in their independent walk with God. I have begun to realize that secure mature people are best described in fifteen words: they know who they are; they like who they are; they are who they are; they are real."

Glenda and I have been married for over thirty years, but it was not until we both took the ***DISC*** personality style analysis, we really came to understand each other. Up until learning about ***DISC***, I felt like a chapter was missing in the rebuilding of our marriage. That chapter is now complete. ***DISC*** is the tool that God put in our lives that is helping us to apply all the other principles He has taught us. Does that mean we have "made it"? Absolutely not! We now have the necessary tool to do as the Apostle Paul wrote in Philippians 3:14 and I paraphrase "We press on toward the goal to have a fulfilling, not problem free, marriage for which God has called us for in Christ Jesus."

Conflict, in my opinion, cannot be dealt with in a positive manner until we gain a clear understanding of not only our personality style blend, but also the style blend of our spouse and children.

If this chapter has inspired you to gain a deeper understanding of your personality style, look in the resource section at the back of the book and it will tell you how to go about purchasing these resources.

Chapter 17

Creating A Marriage Vision

"Where there is no vision, the people are unrestrained." Proverbs 29:18

My marriage was almost destroyed due to the lack vision and so are many other marriages today. The reasons given in part three of this book explains why false visions are often created in marriage. How do we create a common vision for our marriage? Glenda and I went though the following steps, which I adapted, from Harville Hendrix's book, Getting The Love You Want.

- We individually made a list of the qualities we have in the marriage that we wanted to keep.
- We then made a list of the qualities we wished we had in our marriage. If you choose to do this exercise (I encourage you to do so), use positive statements such as, "We can disagree and remain friends."
- We then compared our list. If either of us listed a quality the other did not have, we then added it to our list.
- Next, we individually prioritized each statement by numbering the statement one, two or three, with one being the most important and three being the least important.
- Then individually we circled the two items that were the most important to us.
- Next, we placed a check mark beside the qualities we felt would be the most difficult to achieve.
- Then we got together and designed a mutual marriage vision. We did this by placing an asterisk* by the statements we both agreed were the most important.
- Finally, together we placed a double check mark by the statements we both agreed would be difficult for us to achieve.

Chapter 17 *Creating A Marriage Vision*

I placed my marriage vision in my Bible and I read over it every day in order to keep focused. Periodically, we read our mission statement to each other. I have found this to be a powerful exercise, not only in my marriage, but also in the marriages with which I work.

Think about the company where you work. Regardless of how long ago it was founded, the founder had a vision of what could be accomplished in that business. If it is a thriving business, it is due in part to maintaining not only the original vision, but also expanding that vision. Marriages today are falling apart because the couples have no common vision. I would venture to say that of all the couples you know personally, very few would be able to write out a similar vision statement. I challenge you to create a vision for your marriage and I feel you will be amazed at the difference it will make in your marriage relationship

---

Blair and Glenda Slaughter's Vision:

- A Commitment to rebuild our marriage.
- Seek God's will in all that we do.
- Worship together.
- Develop open and honest communication.
- Recognize, understand and value our differences.
- Give each other quality time.
- Pray together daily.
- Develop our listening skills.
- Develop intimacy: spiritually, emotionally and physically.
- Settle unresolved issues before we go the sleep at night.

Chapter 18

Develop A Mission Statement

When Glenda and I completed our vision statement, we were then able to focus on our marriage and family mission statement. The difference between a vision and a mission statement is a vision is an overall view of what you and your spouse would like your marriage to be. A mission statement gives you a course of action for not only your marriage but also the entire family.

I have heard most of my adult life the importance of having a mission statement. It was not until I worked as training manager for Sears Product Services Marketing Center, I saw first hand the powerful effect a mission statement could have on a group of people. Part of my training was in the area of team building. One exercise we did as a group was developing a mission statement. We not only developed a mission statement, but we put it into to practice in the center. Everything that took place evolved around our mission statement. It was then I saw what a powerful impact a mission statement could have in a marriage and family relationship.

How does one go about developing a mission statement that is not only practical, but has meaning and value? I suggest going through the following steps that I have used with many couples.

- How would you describe the family in athletic terms? A team?
- What is the purpose of a team in competition? To win. In an athletic event, someone has to lose. However, every family can be a winner.
- What are two bottom line characteristics every team must possess in order to win? Commitment and dedication. A team can have the greatest talent and all the resources needed to win but unless there is

Chapter 18 *Develop A Mission Statement*

commitment and dedication, the team will lose.
- What is the ultimate purpose of every family? To honor God?
- Is there anything more important than honoring God within the family team is? Absolutely not!
- Outside of honoring God, is there anything more important than honoring each other within the family team? No.
- Outside of honoring God, each other, is there anything more important honoring other people? No.

When you take that information and put into a statement, it reads as follows: "As a dedicated family team, we are committed to honoring God, each other and other people." That is a powerful mission statement, wouldn't you agree? We have that mission statement matted and framed in our home.

A mission statement is not worth the paper it is written on unless there are steps of action to make it come alive. So, how do we make a mission statement come alive? Answer the following questions by writing your answers on a sheet of paper:

♦ What are you presently doing that shows or demonstrates that you are honoring God?

♦ What are you presently doing that show or demonstrates that you are dishonoring God?

♦ What steps can you take to remove or change the areas that are not honoring God?

♦ What are you presently doing that show or demonstrate that we honor each other as husband, wife, and children?

♦ What are you presently doing that shows or demonstrates that you not honor each other as a husband, wife and children?

I always encourage the husband to initiate these steps of actions by asking his wife first and then each of his children to state how he has dishonored in them in the past. When he has finished, it is the wife's turn to ask her husband and each of the children how she has dishonored them. Then each child, starting with the oldest, asks the parents and siblings how he/she has dishonored them. This is not a very pleasant exercise. One increases respect for each other within the family team.

After each one has finished, the father starts the process all over again by asking his wife then each child what he can do to demonstrate that he honors each of them. Then the wife asks the husband and each child how she can demonstrate she honors each. Then it is the children's turn to ask the parents and siblings how they can demonstrate honor.

What this exercise can lead to is a weekly family conference were individual responsibilities are handed out. After the responsibilities have been assigned, each individual sets their own discipline if they fail to carry any of their responsibilities. What I have found to be true is that children's discipline at times will be more severe than their parent's discipline.

For this exercise to work effectively, parents' discipline must reflect true discipline. One husband set as his discipline not to play golf for one month if he failed to follow through on any of his weekly responsibilities. The response of one child was, "Dad, don't you think that's a little severe?"

That dad failed in one of his responsibilities, applied his own discipline and later told me what a positive affect it had on the entire family.

Developing a mission statement and having a weekly family conference that centers on the mission statement teaches responsibility, accountability and respectability.

Chapter 19

Establish Healthy Communication

What I have found amazing is that a couple can date for several years and talk for what seems like hours, yet after getting married, discover they can't communicate. What is the problem?

In all probability, one of the most dishonest times of our lives is when we were dating our spouse. We make all the sacrifices necessary in order to win their heart. We overlook all the faults and shortcomings. After marriage the sacrifices stop, conflict sets in and the communication barrier suddenly appears. What creates communication barriers? Allow me to mention two:

1. When a husband and wife are not bonded spiritually and emotionally, there will be communication problems (see part III)

2. Many individuals have never been taught some of the basic principles of communication.

In this chapter, I will be sharing some basic principles on communication that the Holy Spirit led me to apply in rebuilding my relationship with my wife and those I have taught to couples.

The two basic principles of healthy communication are listening and hearing. In fact, there will be no communication between a husband and wife unless someone listens. Communication experts tell us that communication consists of 7% words, 38% tone of voice and 55% body language. I have found for most of the couples I've worked with, their communication for the most part is like a dialog with the deaf.

One of the greatest gifts I can give my wife is the gift of listening. In the area of listening, I had to learn the difference between hearing and listening. What is the difference? Hearing is gaining information for my own purposes, whereas listening embodies the quality of empathy toward my wife. Empathy focuses on the thoughts and feelings of my wife. It tells my wife "I really want to understand and help me know if I'm connecting with you."

Hearing means that I am only concerned about what is going on inside me during the conservation, whereas listening means I am trying to understand the feelings of my wife and I am listening for her sake.

Listening is accepting what my wife has to say without judging what is said and how it is being stated. Accepting what my wife has to say does not mean I have to agree with the content of what she says. Rather, it means I understand that what my wife is saying is something she feels is important.

Characteristics of listening:

- I should be able to restate accurately both the content and the feeling of the message.

- It implies that I am interested in my wife's feelings, opinions, and attempt to understand them from her perspective.

- When I listen, I do not get defensive but neither do I have to agree with all that is being said.

- To listen effectively, I must maintain eye contact with my wife.

- I maintain open body language. I do this by not slouching back with crossed arms or legs. Open body language is leaning forward with arms and legs uncrossed.

- My goal is to discover her thoughts and feelings, not to tell her what she is feeling.

What God has taught me is that when I listen to my wife, I step down from being an expert on what my wife really thinks, feels and believes. As one person stated "When I ask you to listen to me and you start giving advice, you have not done what I asked. When I ask you to listen to me and you begin to tell me why I should not feel that way, you are trampling on my feelings. When I ask you to listen to me and you feel you have to do something to solve my problems, you have failed me, strange as that may seem. So please, just listen and hear me. And if you want to talk, wait a few minutes for your turn and I promise I'll listen to you."

Another valuable tool the Lord has taught me in establishing healthy communication with my wife was in the area of language styles. While attending a training seminar on domestic violence, I saw a video by Dr. John

Savage, which explained three basic language styles. Later I read the book *How to Change Your Spouse* by Norman Wright and Gary Oliver, which reiterated much of the same information. What God taught me from these two resources has not only has improved my communication with wife, but has benefited many of the couples with whom I have worked. When I learned to adapt my communication with my wife, it made a tremendous difference.

There are three basic styles. Each style can be described in one word, audio, visual and feeling. Dr. Savage illustrated it this way. There is a committee of three. The chairman says, "On the way to the meeting, it clicked in my mind what the problem is. As you listen to what I tell you about the problem it will click in your mind as well.

The second member says, "I see the problem as not seeing where we have been, where we are and where we are going. What we need are charts showing the people what really needs to be done so they will have a clear picture of the situation.

Third member says, "I don't feel that is the problem at all. What we need is more togetherness, more closeness. We are not in touch with each other, as we need to be.

The chairman responds, "You haven't heard one word I've said."

The second member replies, "That's clear.

The third member says, "You're both out of touch."

What I discovered is that I am a primary visual and secondary feeler. My wife is a primary feeler and secondary audio. It was then I realized that much of our communication problems were because we were speaking different languages.

The audio will use words such as sound, hear, listen, talk, speak, click, tell, call, discuss, loud, tone. The visual will use words such as see, view, diagrams, charts, look, picture, clear, dawn, drawn or draw. The feeler will use words like vibes, touch, feelings happy, unhappy, sad, pressure, hurt, soft, smooth, handle, relax, hard.

The audio wants to hear about life. That is how they learn. The relate more to sounds than sight or feelings. The audio does not notice changes the way the visual notices them.

The visual relates to their surroundings in terms of how things look to him. They visualize and develop pictures of how things should be. The visual is a watcher. They are concerned with how he looks to others. The visual may tend to withdraw and sulk when upset rather than talk through the problem.

Chapter 19 *Establish Healthy Communication*

They prefer face-to-face conversation to using the telephone. The visual responds well to written messages.

Feelers tend to be very feelings oriented. They tend to touch a lot. Often they desire to develop deep relationships. They crave closeness, love and affection. They have the ability to show their feelings without verbalizing them. Their body language reveals their feelings and emotions.

How do we discover what our language style is? Complete the following exercise. You have just witnessed an encounter between a couple at church that could not agree on which restaurant to eat and you were shocked at their behavior. Write out how you would communicate this encounter to your spouse who did not witness this encounter. When you have completed this exercise, examine the type words you used to describe this encounter to your spouse. The result will tell you what your language style is.

To have healthy communication, did I have to change my language style? No. I learned to bridge to my wife's language style. Rather than saying, "Would you like to see a movie," I say, "How do you feel about going a movie?"

A key to healthy communication is for couples to learn to bridge to the language of their spouse. For example, if your spouse is a visual, do not demand that they open up and respond on a feeling level. They have to connect with you on a visual level to feel comfortable. "When you see John leave his family so much, what do you feel?"

If your spouse is an audio, do not expect them to immediately notice that you cleaned the house. He needs to hear about it first. "Honey, I would like to tell you what I went through to get this house cleaned."

The audio may respond, "You cleaned the house?"

What causes a language channel the shut down? Negative messages or wrong life commands that were given to us in our formative years. My audio channel was shut down to life commands such as, "You are to be seen, not heard, Do not talk to me that way, Don't you dare look at me that way, and How dare you to feel that way."

Jeff and Kelly, just retired, came in for counseling. After retirement, they discovered they could not communicate. Both were professional people and their lives had been centered around their professions and raising their children. When I asked them the reason for coming in to see me, Jeff's response was, "We've been married all these years and she's never heard a word I've said."

Kelly responded, "Jeff has never been in touch with my feelings."

Jeff was an audio and Kelly a feeler. I taught them the principles you have just read about and had them to apply them in the session. Jeff told Kelly what he wanted her to hear and she responded back "so what you're telling me is . . .."

Kelly then expressed to Jeff her feelings and Jeff responded back by saying "so what you are feeling is . . .."

When the session ended Jeff said to me, "For the first time, Kelly has finally heard what I had to say."

Kelly responded, "Jeff has finally got in touch with my feelings."

Healthy communication requires being sensitive to and diligently accommodating the uniqueness of our spouse. Adjusting your language style can make the difference between holding your spouse's attention or being ignored.

An easy skill to develop? No. It will take time and commitment to develop healthy communication. It will be an investment with tremendous dividends.

PART SIX:

PARENTING

Chapter 20

Christian Parents - Rebellious Children

> *Ephesians 6:1-4 "Children, obey your parents in the Lord, for this is right. Honor your father and mother, which is the first commandment with a promise. That it may be well with you and you may live long on the earth. And, fathers, do not provoke your children to anger, but bring them up in the discipline and instruction of the Lord."*

In Ephesians chapter 5, verses 22-33, the Apostle Paul wrote concerning the husband – wife relationship. The first four verses of chapter 6, Paul deals with parent – children relationships. Ephesians 6:3 gives a tremendous promise to children and teenagers who honor their parents. The promise is two-fold:

1. Things will go well with them.

2. They may enjoy long life on the earth.

Parents, I challenge you to have your children memorize verses 1 – 3.

Practically every day when you pick up a newspaper, there will be a story of a child killing a parent or some other person. Many Christian parents today are experiencing heartache over kind of life their children are living. This is not a new problem. It had to be one of the problems in the church at Ephesus, or Paul would not have written about it. In fact, the problem did not originate in Ephesus.

One of the most tragic examples of parents provoking the wrath or anger of their children is found in Genesis chapter 27, verses 1-41. Here we have the story of Isaac and Rebekah and the way they raised their twin boys. As you read this story, one would have to conclude that this marriage and family had serious problems. Isaac and Rebekah are not ideal models of parenting. Their parenting skills reflect that something was missing in the dynamics of this family. The scripture points out several things about their parenting that are not healthy for them or their children.

Genesis chapter 25, verse 28 tells us *"And Isaac loved Esau because he ate of his game, but Rebekah loved Jacob."* This verse indicates they played favorites. As we look at the total picture given to us in Genesis, it appears that Rebekah had little to do with Esau and Isaac had little to do with Jacob. It appears that when Jacob did not measure up to Isaac's expectations, he rejected him. When Esau did not measure up to Rebekah's expectations, she rejected him. These twin boys never had the unconditional acceptance of their parents. Many parents make the same mistake today and provoke wrath or anger in their child or children. Our society itself is actually encouraging more and more favoritism in it emphasis on visible markers of success. All are created for unconditional acceptance.

When a parent or parents develop expectations for a son or daughter and for some reason that son or daughter does not meet those expectations, those parents may consciously or unconsciously reject their child. Dr. Rohm tells the story of a young lady whose mother kept pressuring her to make better grades. When she finally made an A+, the mother only said, "You could have taken a harder course."

That is inferred rejection and it belittles the child's accomplishment.

I have counseled many adults who never felt they measured up to their parent's expectations, which created many problems in their marriage and family relationships.

Let us look back at how the favoritism of Isaac and Rebekah evolves. Genesis chapter 27 verses 6-13, *"Rebekah said to her son Jacob, 'Behold, I heard your father speak to your brother Esau, saying, 'Bring me some game and prepare a savory dish for me, that I may eat, and bless you in the presence of the Lord before my death.' 'Now therefore, my son, listen to me as I command you. Go now to the flock and bring me two choice kids from there, that I may prepare them, as savory dish for your father, such as he loves. Then you shall bring it to your father, that he may eat, so that he may bless you before his death.' And Jacob answered his mother Rebekah, 'Behold, Esau my brother is a hairy man, and I am a smooth man. Perhaps my father will feel me, then I shall be as a deceiver in his sight; and I shall bring upon myself a curse and not a blessing.' But his mother said to him, 'your curse be on me, my son; only obey my voice, and go, get them for me.'"*

Three things stand out in this story:

1. Rebekah was selfish. She did not care about Isaac or Esau. She wanted "her" Jacob to get the blessing. We will never know why, but this might have been her unhealthy reaction to Isaac's withdrawal from the family once he had obtained his first born, Esau.

2. She did not care about the consequences of her actions. Verse 13 *"Let your curse be on me, my son; only obey my voice, and go get them for me."* I am afraid there are many parents today who do not care about the consequences of their actions as parents and use their children to act out their problems. The consequences of sin are far greater than we can ever imagine when we choose to violate God's principles.

3. Jacob in turn grew up to be selfish, and weak in character. Jacob was so weak in character that he lied to his father 4 times because Rebekah said so, even though he knew it was wrong.

Lie # 1: Genesis 27:19a *"And Jacob said to his father, I am Esau your firstborn."*

Lie # 2: Genesis 27:19b *"I have done just as you told me; please arise, sit and eat of my game, that your soul may bless me."* Jacob again did as Rebekah said. Financial gain is and always has been a strong motivation for some.

Lie # 3: Genesis 27:20 *" ... And Jacob said, because the Lord your God brought it to me."* God had nothing to do with it.

Lie # 4: Genesis 27:24 *"Then Isaac said, are you really my son Esau? And Jacob said, I am."* What a sad reflection of Isaac's uninvolved parenting - that he did not truly know either of his sons. This account confirms the lack of interaction between Jacob and his father and Esau and his mother.

Rebekah smothered and was over protective of Jacob and he did just as she said. Jacob had no internal value system. His mother set the value system and Jacob played along.

Children need their father's influence in their life. The Apostle had a reason for saying, *"Fathers provoke not your children to wrath or anger."* Jacob did not have positive direction from his father, teaching him his role and responsibilities as a future family head. Esau also did not benefit by his father's unhealthy favoritism.

Every child also needs the nurturing love of his/her mother. I do not believe Esau or Jacob ever had the true nurturing love of his mother. Nurturing love develops each individual to their full potential, including and accepting differences. Nurturing love does not smother one and neglect another, preventing either from a proper development.

Notice the results of the inconsistency of Isaac and Rebekah's parenting. Esau carried a grudge against Jacob and planned to kill him after Isaac died. As a result, Jacob had to flee and leave his mother. Can you imagine what Jacob must have felt when he was forced to leave his mother? Can you imagine also the resentment and bitterness that Esau must have carried around?

Isaac and Rebekah both experienced heartache and a broken heart because of their parenting. Isaac's was because he knew his son lied to him and Rebekah's because she never saw Jacob again. As you study the life of Jacob, you will discover that his own sons deceive him just as he deceived his father, only in a different manner.

Many Christian parents today are experiencing heartache because of their parenting or lack of parenting. They see their child or children go into their teens and rebel against everything they tried to teach them. Why? Hosea chapter 4, verse 6 is one answer *"For my people are destroyed from a lack of knowledge."* Many parents lack the proper knowledge in how to parent. Some parents have done all the right things and the child still goes bad. I have no answer for that. The purpose is to present principles to help you be more effective in your parenting.

Diana Baumrind has done extensive research on parenting and her results have revealed that certain types of parenting produce certain types of children. She states that there are 3 types of parenting styles:

Authoritarian, Permissive, and Authoritative.

1. Authoritarian Parenting Style:

The majorities who fall into this parenting style are fundamental and conservation Christian parents. In my opinion, this is not a biblical model. Characteristics of this parenting style include:

- Attempting to control the child in their attitudes and behavior.
- They have a set of standards of behavior, which are usually absolute standards.
- The have a solid ideal of what is good or bad for the child, regardless of the child's personality.
- They are not flexible and will not negotiate, even when the child is close to adulthood.
- Will use forceful methods to control the child.
- Emphasizes respect for authority and are conservative and traditional.
- They do not engage in verbal give and take with the child, and do not seek the child's input.

This parenting style works well with small children and can produce a well-behaved child, but does not work with teens and can produce rebellious and defiant teenagers.

2. The Permissive (liberal) Parenting Style:

- They are non-punitive. The are not quick to punish or discipline.
  They are very patient. "I love you regardless. Please don't do that anymore."
- They consult with the child on policy decisions. The child is involved and often is allowed the final choice, even when inappropriate.
- Very few demands made on the child. They allow the child or teen determine appropriate levels of responsibility.
- The child is allowed to regulate their behavior. "He'll go to bed when he is tired" or "He will eventually come."
- Will attempt to use reason but will not overpower to accomplish parental goals.

The authoritarian parent and the permissive, parent share couple of things in common. First, they produce children who do not possess an internal value system as to why they should or should not behave in a certain manner. The child or teenager does or does not do because of external or outside forces. Second, they both produce children or teenagers who have never learned how to accept responsibility for thinking through their own responses to situations and reaping the logical consequences.

Many Christian parents who are good Godly people raise their children who when they become teenagers, totally reject the value system of their parents because that value system was never internalized or decided on by the teenager. Often, they do not realize that imposing a value system or showing a value system is not the same as teaching the child the value system. The child must be allowed to explore both good and bad consequences of the value system to internalize it.

I recall the story I heard of the young man who was elected be president of bank upon the retirement of the present president. The young man met with the retiring president and asked him for advice in not only maintaining the banks present position but also leading the bank to newer heights.

The retiring president responded, "Make good decisions."

The young man replied, "How do I make good decisions?"

The retiring president said, "Experience."

The young man then said, "Sir, I appreciate that, but that doesn't help me very much. How do I get experience?"

The retiring president answered, "Make bad decisions."

The young man replied, "Sir, I thank you for your advice. With it I can be successful."

3. The Authoritative Parenting Style:

This is the closest to a biblical model.

- Attempts to direct the child in a rational issues-oriented manner. They focus on the child's potential.

- Verbal give and take is encouraged as age appropriate. The parent is willing to talk things over not in a threatening way but in hopes of getting the child or teenage to do the right thing.

- Will lead rather than dictate or dominate. They will give reasons or explanations for the rules. They avoid using the phrase, "Because I said so."

- The parent values expressive attributes, independence and creativity. The Authoritarian confuses independence with rebellion. Independence is developed through giving the positives and negatives and holding the child or teenage responsible and accountable for his or her choices.

- Will exert firm control at points where there is a difference in opinion, but is not overly restrictive. The parent is not afraid to use their authority to protect their child from harm.

- Will use reason as well as power to achieve objective.

- They recognize that both children and parents have rights, and these can be found in the Bible.

The philosophy of the authoritative parent is like Joshua's "as for me and my house we will serve the Lord."

Parenting skills can only be judged when children are grown, having a family on their own, not when they are children or teenagers.

Parents can provoke the wrath their children by developing one or more of the following negative parent-child interaction patterns.

- ▶ Threatening, dominating and controlling their child or teenager.

- ▶ Being overly permissive, this can result in a child or teenager who expects over gratification without effort. The child who has been given everything without responsibility and accountability thinks the world owes them a living. They tend to be thrill seeking and have very poor self-discipline or self-control.

- Over protective parents produce fearful, self-doubting children or teenagers. Their curiosity is stifled and they develop low self-esteem. They become rebellious at their parents because they recognize they have been made this way.

- When parents fail to accept a child when he or she does not meet their expectations, they tend to rebel inwardly or outwardly, depending on their personality style. The message to the child or teenager is conditional love and acceptance.

- Distrustful parents will produce a child or teenager who will be untrustworthy.

- Inconsistency. Children can tolerate almost anything except inconsistency. They become frustrated, anxious, withdrawn and this is a reason many leave home. They do not know what to believe or expect.

- Neglectful parents produce children of low self-esteem. It is very difficult for them to step out and take charge.

Parents, your children and my children are a reflection of our parenting. We need to take a close look at our parenting skills and make adjustments where needed. We need to ask and give the Holy Spirit permission to reveal where and how we can improve our parenting. If we have made mistakes, as we all do, ask the Lord to forgive us where we failed. Then ask our children for their forgiveness. Remember, being or becoming a Christian does not mean instant parenting success. Parenting, as any other skill, takes knowledge and practice. Being a Christian simply means that we do have the Bible to use as a standard, and we have the Lord to forgive us and guide us when we ask.

Chapter 21

Guarding Your Children from Moral Impurity

Sandy, a fifteen year old, said to me "Why don't my parents love me enough to tell me no?"

Before answering her question, I inquired about her parents. She revealed they were "good" people, Christians and active in their church. They always took her to church and taught her about the Bible.

I questioned, "Are you telling me your parents have allowed to do whatever you decided?"

Her response was, "Yes. It seems to me they were afraid they would hurt my feelings if they told me no."

I then asked, "Are you telling me you wished they would tell you, no?"

Sandy replied, "I wished they had no told me no."

I questioned her further, "What do you mean by 'had told you no?'"

With tears in her eyes she said, "If they would have set to limits or restrictions, I wouldn't be in trouble today."

I responded by asking, "What kind of trouble are you in?"

She replied, "I'm pregnant and I've got to tell my parents when I get home. Will you pray for me and my parents?"

Many Christian parents today are heart broken due to immoral choices their children have made, practically ruining their lives. Children are provoked to anger or wrath when parents fail to teach them, show them and see that they follow after the principles and commands of God that are found in the Bible. Many dads and moms today have the love of their children but not their respect. **There is a difference!**

One of the many responsibilities parents have is to guard and protect our children from evil and moral impurity. There is no set formula to guarantee a child will be morally pure. However, I will give you thirteen steps that, when applied, may help you raise morally pure children who will shun evil, thus fulfilling Paul's command in Ephesians 6:4, *"Fathers, do not irritate and provoke your children to anger (do not exasperate them to resentment), but rear them (tenderly) in the training and discipline and the counsel and admonition of the Lord."* (AMP)

These steps were developed from individuals with whom I have worked who experienced moral difficulty in their lives. In each situation, some or all of the thirteen steps presented were never a part of their relationship with their parents.

1. Dedicate your children to God. Not only dedicate them to the Lord, but also throughout their life remind them they belong to God. Remind them periodically that God is holding you accountable in the way you parent them.

2. Lead them to salvation, a personal relationship with Jesus Christ.

3. Let your words, attitudes and actions demonstrate that your purpose in life is to be pleasing to God in all that you do and in the best interest of your family. The only way you can accomplish this purpose is to spend time daily with the Lord in prayer and Bible study.

4. When your child or teenage disappoints or disobeys you, let them see how they have wounded you in your spirit rather than seeing and hearing anger. Shannon, my oldest daughter, was caught being disobedient. I brought into the den and had her sit beside me on the sofa. I told her disappointed I was in her behavior. She responded, "Daddy, I'm sorry. I will not do it again. May I go back to my room?"

I said, 'no'.

Again I emphasized to her how disappointed and hurt I was in her behavior. After a few moments of silence, Shannon with tears in his eyes said, "Daddy, I didn't mean to disappoint and hurt you. I'm really sorry." With a hug she added, "Please forgive me." I forgave her.

The majority of adults with whom I have worked, when asked what the attitude of the parent was when being punished was that of anger. Punishment or discipline given in anger is the breeding ground for resentment and bitterness, which leads to rebellion.

5. Teach your children to fear God. I believe it was Henry Blackaby who said, "The seminar that is needed in the church today is to fear God." As parents, we should teach our children that God is constantly aware of every action is always watching and evaluating everything that he/she says, does and thinks.

One of the best ways to teach children is to fear God is to have them memorize scripture. If I could turn back the clock on my parenting, in addition to the scripture I had them memorize, I would also had them to memorize the following scriptures:

Psalms 139: 1-12 *"O Lord, you have searched me (thoroughly) and have know me. You know my down sitting and my uprising; You understand my thought afar off. You sift and search out my path and my lying down, and You are acquainted with all my ways. For there is not a word in my tongue (still unuttered), but, behold, O Lord, You know it altogether. You have beset me and shut me in-behind and before, and You have laid Your hand upon me. Your (infinite) knowledge is too wonderful for me - it is high above me, I cannot reach it. Where could I go from Your Spirit? On the other hand, where could I flee from Your presence? If I ascend into heaven, You are there; if I make my bed in Sheol, behold you are there. If I take the wings of the morning or dwell in the uttermost parts of the sea, even there shall Your hand lead me, and Your right hand shall hold me. If I say, 'Surely the darkness shall cover me and the night shall be (the only) light about me, even the darkness hides nothing from You, but the night shines as the day; the darkness and the light are both alike to You.'"* (AMP)

Proverbs 8:13 *"The fear of the Lord is to hate evil; Pride and arrogance and the evil way and the perverted mouth, I hate."*

Proverbs 15:3 *"The eyes of the Lord are everywhere, keeping watch on the wicked and the good."*

II Corinthians 5:10 *"For we must all appear before the judgment seat of Christ, that each one may receive what is due him for the things done while in the body, whether good or bad."*

Psalms 94:9 *"Does He who implanted the ear not hear? Does He who formed the eye not see?"*

Proverbs 5:21 *"For a man's ways are in full view of the Lord, and He examines all his paths."*

Proverbs 9:10 *"The fear of the Lord is the beginning of wisdom, and knowledge of the Holy One is understanding."*

Proverbs 16:6 *"By mercy and truth iniquity is purged: and by fear of the Lord men depart from evil."*

How do we inspire our children to be motivated to memorize scripture? That is the sixth step to help guard your children from evil and moral impurity.

6. Reward you children for building character, not for doing chores around the house. Reward your children for . . ..

- Every verse of scripture they memorize.
- For every chapter they read in Proverbs and writing a summary of the chapter read.
- For reading books that build character and for writing a book report.

7. Give them a sense of destiny, that God has a plan and purpose for their lives.

Jim Sunburg, former catcher for the Texas Rangers and the Kansas City Royals, tells the following story:

> I was visiting a prison one day, sharing a word of encouragement with the inmates. I told them when I was a boy, my father and I would play catch in the afternoon. One day, I threw the ball over his head and thought I was in trouble. But my dad said, "Son, anybody who can throw a ball that far is going to play in the big leagues one day." Another time, my father pitched the ball to me and I swung as hard as I could, but missed. My father looked at me and said, "Son, anybody who can swing a bat that hard is going to play in the big leagues one day. And another time, I hit the ball over the fence, through the neighbor's plate glass window. My dad said, "Son, anybody who can hit a ball like that is going to play in the big leagues one day." When I grew up, there was nothing left for me to do but play in the big leagues!

Jim continued, "After I finished speaking, a man came up to me who had chains around his ankles. He said, 'Mr. Sunburg, I had a dad sort of like yours. He told me I was no good and that I would never amount to anything, and one day I would end up in prison. I fulfilled his dreams for me, too.'" How important it is that we share words of encouragement and build confidence in those around us, especially our youth.

My dad gave me a sense of destiny by reminding me throughout my childhood and teenage years that God created me for a unique calling in my life. He prayed that God would call me into the ministry if it were His will. Did I become a minister to please my dad? Absolutely not. There has never been a time in my life where I doubted God's call into the ministry.

8. Show them the consequences of sin. Take them on tour of a prison unit. Have them visit a crisis pregnancy center and talk to unwed mothers. Allow the to see inside a juvenile detention center. Show your children the consequences of wrong choices.

9. Admit when you are wrong. In one of my seminars I ask the audience to close their eyes and then ask this question, "How many of you ever heard your dad admit he was wrong and the ask for your forgiveness?" Only a couple of individuals raised their hands. In those moments of reflection, several in the audience began to weep. They were still carrying the hurt and pain of the dad who never had the courage to say, "I was wrong." Parents, what are you teaching your children by never admitting when you are wrong? This is a fact, when you are wrong, your children know it whether you admit it or not. By never admitting when you are wrong, you are teaching your children never to take responsibility for their wrong actions.

10. Teach them to set healthy boundaries in their lives by establishing healthy boundaries in your marriage and family. I encourage you to read *Boundaries in Marriage and Boundaries with Kids* by Henry Cloud and John Townsend.

11. Be a Proverbs 22:6 parent, *"Train up a child in the way he should go, even when he is old he will not depart from it."* The literal translation is *"Train [start] a child according to his [the child's] way."* Parents have the responsibility to discover the unique personality traits of their children and raise them accordingly. Many parents raise their children in the way they see themselves. This may work if the child has a similar personality as the parent. Personality traits vary in each child. When a parent fails to recognize these varying traits, problems will arise. In the resource section at the back of the book, you will find listed their resources that will help you in determining the personality style or blend for your children.

12. When they have tried and failed, praise them, and then show them how they can improve the next time around. Show them how to correct their mistakes. Share experiences where you have failed and how you learned from your failure. Failure is not final. Failure is only final when a person dies without Jesus Christ and goes to hell. Until that point, there is always a second chance.

13. Pray a blessing on and with each child every day. This will only require a few seconds of your time and will pay huge dividends. Not only pray a blessing on each child but on your wife as well. What does this accomplish? They are aware of God's presence with them throughout the day.

These thirteen steps are by no means complete. There are other steps parents could probably take to help guard or protect their children from moral impurity.

The first institution God established was marriage and the family. Christ's first miracle was at a wedding. One of the last events to occur is the marriage supper of the Lamb. Throughout the Bible, our relationship with the Lord is described as a marriage. Christ is the groom and we the believers are His brides. What does all that mean? As Bill Gothard wrote, "Marriage (and family) is like a classroom in which Christ teaches us His character, in which He teaches us the qualities that we need to develop in our lives. Your marriage (and family) relationship will force you to judge or reveal:

▶ If your love is stronger than the hateful words or actions that may have been given to you.

▶ Whether or not your joy is able to withstand the adversities of life;

▶ Whether or not our inward peace can remain steady in the midst of turmoil.

▶ Whether or not our long-suffering is wise enough to forgive our partner or children when he/she offends us.

▶ Whether or not our goodness is genuine enough to keep on giving to the needs of our spouse or children when there is nothing to be gained in returned.

▶ Whether or not our gentleness demonstrates a continuing sensitivity to the needs of our spouse and children..

▶ Whether or not our faith is strong enough to see how God is causing all things to work together for our good by conforming us to the image of Christ.

▶ Whether or not our meekness reveals that we have truly given all of our lives - all of our rights to God.

▶ Whether or not our self-control is able to show itself in our words, actions, thoughts and attitudes.

▶ When we withdraw our spirit from our spouse or children or if we react negatively, or with bad attitude when corrected or confronted, we are cutting off all the vital character-building techniques that God is wanting to us to shape and mold our character.

A successful marriage and family relationship – a fantasy or reality? It can be a reality if we are willing to allow the Holy Spirit to convict us and be obedient to the principles He wants us to apply in our relationships.

ABOUT W. BLAIR SLAUGHTER, JR.

Received his A.B. degree from Southern Wesleyan University and His M.A. in counseling from Liberty University.

Founder and president of Cornerstone Marriage Ministries in High Point, North Carolina.

Served in the pastoral ministry for over 25 years.

Led and conducted workshops and seminars for churches, organizations and businesses.

Certified Human Behavior Consultant in DISC training, affiliated with Personality Insight, Inc., Atlanta, GA.

Worked with and counseled hundreds of couples who have experienced marital and family difficulty.

Produced a video series on Building A Strong Marriage and Family.

Produced a sixteen-week television series on Building A Strong Marriage and Family, which aired on WLXI, Greensboro, NC, February – May 1995.

If you would be interested in having Blair Slaughter speak to your church on Building A Strong Marriage and Family; or to your business on Building Better Team Relationships, you can contact him at Cornerstone Marriage Ministries, P.O. Box 5721, High Point, NC 27262, Phone 336-887-2664.

RESOURCES

Anderson, Neil T. *The Seven Steps To Freedom*. Gospel Light. 1996.

Boyd, Charles R. *Different Children Different Needs*. Sisters, Oregon. Multnomah Books. 1994.

Chapman, Gary. *The Five Love Languages*. Chicago, Illinois. Northfield Publishing. 1992.

Cloud, Henry and John Townsend. *Boundaries In Marriage*. Grand Rapids, Michigan. Zondervan Publishing House. 1992.

Cloud, Henry and John Townsend. *Boundaries With Kids*. Grand Rapids, Michigan. Zondervan Publishing House. 1998.

Engstrom, Ted. *The Making Of A Christian Leader*. Grand Rapids, Michigan. Zondervan Publishing House. 1976.

Engstrom, Ted and Edward Dayton. *Lectures From Managing Your Time*, A MARC Seminar. Monrovia, California.

Gothard, Bill. *Lecturer from the Institute in Basic Youth Conflicts*. Oakbrook, Illinois.

Hancock, Maxine and Karen Burton Mains. *Child Sexual Abuse: A Hope for Healing*. Wheaton, Illinois. Harold Shaw. 1987.

Harley, Willard F., Jr. *His Needs, Her Needs*. Old Tappen, New Jersey. Fleming H. Revell Company. 1986.

Harley, Willard F., Jr. *Love Busters*. Old Tappen, New Jersey. Fleming H. Revell Company. 1992.

Hegstrom, Paul. *Lecturer from Learning To Live*, Learning to Love Center. Quincy, Illinois.

Hemfelt, Robert, Frank Minirth and Paul Meier. *Love Is A Choice*. Nashville, Tennessee. Thomas Nelson Publishers. 1989.

Hemfelt, Robert, Frank Minirth and Paul Meier. *We Are Driven*. Nashville, Tennessee. Thomas Nelson Publishers. 1991.

Kimmel, Tim. *Little House On The Freeway*. Multnomah Press. Portland, Oregon. 1987.

Maxwell, John. *Developing The Leader Within You*. Nashville, Tennessee. Thomas Nelson Publishers. 1993.

Rohm, Robert A. *Positive Personality Profiles*. Atlanta. Georgia. Personality Insights Inc. 1997.

Rohm, Robert A. *Who Do You Think You Are . . . Anyway?* Atlanta, Georgia. Personality Insights Inc. 1997.

Smalley, Gary. *Hidden Keys To Loving Relationships.*. Paoli, Pennsylvania. Relationships Today, Inc. 1988.

Smalley, Gary. *For Better Or For Best*. Zondervan Publishing House. Grand Rapids, Michigan. 1987.

Smalley, Gary and John Trent. *Home Remedies*. Multnomah Press. Portland, Oregon. 1991.

Smalley, Gary. *If He Only Knew*. Zondervan Publishing House. Grand Rapids, Michigan. 1987.

NOW AVAILABLE ON VIDEO

This is a 12-week course that covers the major issues presented in the book. This is an excellent resource that can be used in Sunday school or small groups. There are four videotapes, accompanied by a facilitator's guide.

These videos are currently being used during Sunday school at Green Street Baptist Church, High Point, NC. Here is what Frank Hensley, Minister of Education has to say:

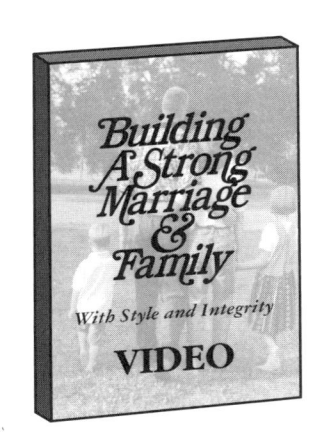

"Building a Strong Marriage and Family has become a foundational discipleship class for our church. Offered in a closed group setting, this twelve-week breakout class has become one of the most demanded classes we have. Couples have the opportunity to come out of their regular Bible study class on Sunday morning for one quarter and then return after the completion of this class. We have been offering this class for a year and approximately fifty couples have taken advantage of it.

Blair Slaughter of *Cornerstone Ministries* has put together a video based program that will meet the needs of any couple that wants to strengthen their marriage relationship and improve the life of their family.

I wholeheartedly recommend this program to any church that wants to provide an alternative to the secular approach that is offered to most marriage and family relationships. This program is Bible based and has Christ as the cornerstone."

To obtain further information on this video series, visited our web site:

www.cornerstonemm.com

Or, you may write: Blair Slaughter, Cornerstone Marriage Ministries, P.O. Box 5721, High Point, NC 27262. Phone: 336-887-2664.

ORDER FORM

your name - *please print legibly!*

your mailing address — *street or post office box*

your city, state, zip code   telephone number

credit card number (if charging)   expiration date   name on card

e-mail aderess

Quantity	Description	Unit Price	TOTAL

BOOKS   *(Prices subject to changes)*

_____ Building A Strong Marriage & Family (book) 12.95 _____
_____ Positive Personality Profiles (book)   12.95 _____
_____ Different Children Different Needs (book)   12.95 _____
_____ Tales Out of School (book)   12.95 _____
_____ Who Do You Think You Are Anyway? (book)   14.95 _____
_____ You've Got Style (book)   11.95 _____
_____ Understanding How Others Misunderstand You (book) 15.95 _____

SELF-SCORING PROFILES

_____ Self-Scoring Adult Profile   10.00 _____
_____ Self-Scoring Teen Profile (with cassette tape)   10.00 _____
_____ Self-Scoring Child Profile (with cassette tape)   10.00 _____

                                SUBTOTAL $ _____

NORTH CAROLINA RESIDENTS ADD 6.5% Sales Tax $ _____
ADD 10% OF SUBTOTAL FOR SHIPPING AND HANDLING $ _____
TOTAL BY CHECK OR CREDIT CARD $ _____

If you are paying by check, please make payable in U.S. funds to:
Cornerstone Marriage Ministries
P.O. Box 5721 High Point, NC 27262-5721 • 336-887-2664
or visit our website at http://www.cornerstonemm.com